TWAYNE'S WORLD AUTHORS SERIES

A Survey of the World's Literature

Sylvia E. Bowman, Indiana University

GENERAL EDITOR

GERMANY

Ulrich Weisstein, Indiana University

EDITOR

Franz Kafka

TWAS 381

Franz Kafka

FRANZ KAFKA

By MENO SPANN

Northwestern University

TWAYNE PUBLISHERS
A Division of G. K. Hall & Co.
Boston, Massachusetts, U. S. A.

1976

Library of Congress Cataloging in Publication Data

Spann, Meno, 1903–
    Franz Kafka.

    Twayne's world authors series ; TWAS 381 : Germany)
    Bibliography: pp. 195–200
    Includes index.
    1. Kafka, Franz, 1883–1924.
PT 2621.A26Z877   833'.9'12 [B]   75–26548
ISBN 0–8057–6182–9

Contents

About the Author

Meno Spann was born in 1903 in Koblenz, Germany. He attended the *Gymnasium* in Hannover until 1922. From 1922–28 he studied German literature, philology and philosophy at the universities of Göttingen, Berlin and Marburg, receiving the Ph.D. degree from the University of Marburg (1928). He then began his teaching career in the United States as Instructor in the German Department of Cornell University. He has also held teaching positions at the University of Oregon, the University of North Carolina, the University of Maryland and the University of Iowa. From 1943–71 he taught at Northwestern University, which he left as Professor Emeritus. In the 1971–72 academic year, he served as Visiting Professor in the German Department of Michigan State University. Spann became an American citizen in 1936.

As author and coauthor, Dr. Spann has published several German grammars and other German textbooks. In his scholarly work his fields of interest encompassed German romanticism, Heinrich Heine, Goethe, Rilke, Thomas Mann and Franz Kafka. He has contributed articles to various German journals about these writers, particularly Kafka, and has written a book on Heinrich Heine.

Preface

Two decades of studying and teaching Kafka, of writing and reading about him, have taught the author that the extended metaphors in the work of this great writer express the complex feelings of a highly sensitive modern man harassed by ancient and modern ills. To this reader, the works of Kafka do not seem to be, as the majority of critics asserts, religious or existential allegories, visions of Armageddon, or laments of a misunderstood artist. What psychoanalyzing critics have revealed about Kafka's neuroses appears to be irrelevant to the intentions he realized in his stories.

In 1966 the West Berlin *Akademie der Künste* sponsored a number of literary symposia in which international scholars discussed the necessity of revising the Kafka image which the allegorizing critics had created. The demands for a renewed study of Kafka, made during these sessions, inspired this book.

Throughout, quotations from Kafka's works, letters, diaries, and conversations are taken from the standard translations, passages from *Franz Kafka: Briefe* (Letters) were translated by the author.

MENO SPANN

Northwestern University

Acknowledgments

Reprinted by permission of Basic Books, Inc. from *The Terror of Art: Kafka and Modern Literature*, by Martin Greenberg. Copyright © 1965, 1966, 1968 by Martin Greenberg.

Reprinted by permission of Cambridge University Press from *Franz Kafka*, by Ronald Gray. Copyright © 1973 by Cambridge University Press.

Reprinted by permission of Cambridge University Press from *Franz Kafka: Der Heizer, in der Strafkolonie, der Bau*, with introduction and notes by J. M. S. Pasley. Copyright © 1966 by Cambridge University Press.

Reprinted by permission of S. Fischer Verlag from *Conversations With Kafka*, by Gustav Janouch, translated by Goronwy Rees. Copyright © 1968 by S. Fischer Verlag GmbH, Frankfurt a.M.

Reprinted by permission of Cornell University Press from *Franz Kafka: Parable and Paradox*, by Heinz Politzer. Copyright © 1962, 1966 by Cornell University Press.

Reprinted by permission of A. Francke Verlag from *Kafkas Dichtungen: Die Travestien des Mythos*, by Kurt Weinberg. Copyright © 1963 by A. Francke Verlag.

Reprinted by permission of Alfred A. Knopf from *The Castle* by Franz Kafka, translated by Willa and Edwin Muir, with additional material translated by Eithne Wilkins and Ernst Kaiser. Copyright © 1930, 1958 by Alfred A. Knopf, Inc.

Reprinted by permission of Alfred A. Knopf, Inc. from *The Trial*, by Franz Kafka, translated by Willa and Edwin Muir,

Acknowledgments

Chronology

1883 Franz Kafka born in Prague, July 3, son of Herrmann (1852–1931) and Julie (née Löwy, 1856–1934).

1885, Brothers Georg and Heinrich born. Both die in infancy.
1887

1889– Attends German elementary school on the Fleischmarkt.
1893

1889, Sisters Gabriele (Elli) and Valerie (Valli) born.
1890

1892 Sister Ottilie (Ottla) born.

1893– Attends German Gymnasium on the Altstädter Ring.
1901 Friendship Oskar Pollak, Hugo Bergmann. Reads Spinoza, Darwin, Haeckel, Nietzsche.

1899– Early writings (destroyed).
1903

1901– Studies chemistry (two weeks), then law at the German
1906 Karl-Ferdinand University in Prague.

1902 In the summer term, he studies German literature. Vacation at the home of his favorite uncle, Dr. Siegfried Löwy (the country doctor) in Triesch, Moravia. First meeting with Max Brod.

1904 Writes *Beschreibung eines Kampfes*.

1905 In Zuckmantel, at the foot of the Sudeten, love affair with an unnamed woman. First regular meetings with Max Brod, the writer Oskar Baum and the philosopher Felix Weltsch.

1906 Doctorate in jurisprudence from the German University, Prague. Writes *Hochzeitsvorbereitungen auf dem Lande*. In October he begins the prescribed year of practical legal experience, first in a district court, then in a criminal court.

1907 In October, he is hired by the Assicurazioni Generali, an Italian insurance company, in Prague.

1908　February to May: course in workers' insurance at the Commercial Academy in Prague. In July he begins to work for the Workers' Accident Insurance Office for the Kingdom of Bohemia in Prague. He remains with the firm until his retirement in 1922, rising from probationer to senior secretary. Eight sketches from the collection *Betrachtung* published in *Hyperion*, a journal edited by Franz Blei. Reads with Brod Plato (in Greek), Huysmans, Flaubert, Robert Walser, Kleist, Hamsun.

1909　September: In Riva and Breschia with Max and Otto Brod. "Die Aeroplane in Brescia" published in *Bohemia*. The two "Gespräche" (from *Beschreibung eines Kampfes*) published in *Hyperion*.

1910　Begins his diary. Attends evening lectures given at the Fanta House on Hegel, Fichte, Einstein, Planck, Freud, Rudolf Steiner. Visits Paris with Max and Otto Brod. Begins, jointly with Max Brod, the novel *Richard und Samuel*.

1911　Visits Warnsdorf in the Sudeten Mountains. In August travels to North Italian lakes (Lugano, Stresa) with Max Brod, and then to Paris. Deeply moved by the Yiddish theater company which performed in the café Savoy. Friendship with the Yiddish actor Jizchak Löwy.

1912　February: *Rede über die Jiddische Sprache*. Studies Judaism. Winter and spring: first version of *Amerika*. July: vacation with Max Brod in Weimar (Goethe pilgrimage), then alone at Jungborn, a nature healing sanatorium in the Harz mountains. August: readies his first book, *Betrachtung*, for publication. Meets Felice Bauer at Brod's home. September: writes "Das Urteil." September 20: begins correspondence with Felice Bauer. September, 1912, until January, 1913, the first seven chapters of the second version of *Amerika*. November and December: writes "Die Verwandlung." *Betrachtung* published.

1913　Easter: first visit to Felice Bauer in Berlin. April: works in a garden-complex in Troja, near Prague. May: second visit to Felice in Berlin. "Der Heizer" (first chapter of *Amerika*) published. September: visits Vienna, Venice, and Riva. Meets "the Swiss girl."

Chronology

1914   April 12: first engagement to Felice. July 12: first disengagement. Begins to write his novel *Der Prozess*. October: "In der Strafkolonie" written in two weeks.

1915   Meets Felice in Bodenbach. Visits Hungary. Carl Sternheim gives the money from his Fontane Prize to Kafka. November: "Die Verwandlung" published.

1916   July: stays with Felice in Marienbad. September: "Das Urteil" published. Publicly reads "In der Strafkolonie" in Munich. In Ottla's room in the Alchimistengasse most stories of *Landarzt* cycle are written.

1917   *Landarzt* cycle finished. In March he takes a two-room apartment in the Schönborn Palace. July: second engagement to Felice (second and final disengagement in December). Studies Hebrew. September: tuberculosis of the lungs diagnosed. Moves to Zürau, where he stays with his sister Ottla. Reads Kierkegaard. Writes aphorisms.

1918   At Zürau. Returns to Prague in the summer. Winter spent at Schelesen, north of Prague. Meets Julie Wohryzek.

1919   Spring: returns to Prague. Engagement to Julie. "Letter to his Father." "In der Strafkolonie," *Ein Landarzt* published.

1920   Cure taken in Merano. Meets Milena Jesenska-Polak and Gustav Janouch. Engagement with Julie Wohryzek broken off. December: enters the sanatorium at Matliary in the Tatra mountains. Beginning of friendship with the young medical student Robert Klopstock.

1921   Matliary. Autumn: back in Prague. Gives his diaries to Milena.

1922   January and February: in Spindlermühle. Writes *Das Schloss* (January to September), in the spring "Ein Hungerkünstler," in the summer "Forschungen eines Hundes." July: retires from the insurance office. From end of June to September: in Planá with sister Ottla. "Hungerkünstler" published in *Die Neue Rundschau*.

1923   With sister Elli in Müritz on the Baltic Sea. Meets Dora Diamant, lives with her in Berlin. October: writes "Eine Kleine Frau," in the winter: *Der Bau*.

1924   Tuberculosis worsens, in March back to Prague. Spring: writes "Josefine die Sängerin." With Dora Diamant and

Robert Klopstock in sanatorium at Kierling, near Vienna, where he dies June 3. Funeral in Prague, June 11. Collection *Ein Hungerkünstler* published in summer.

1942 Death of sister Ottla in Auschwitz. Elli and Walli also perish in concentration camps.

1944 Grete Bloch killed during Nazi occupation of Italy. Milena dies in Ravensbrück, a concentration camp for women.

1952 Death of Dora Diamant in London.

1960 Death of Felice Bauer in New York.

1968 Death of Max Brod in Tel Aviv.

CHAPTER 1

Educators

I Drillmasters

THE German-Austrian writer Franz Kafka lived a tragic existence the external reasons for which are furnished by the simple biographical statement: he was born in 1883 in the German-Jewish enclave of Prague as the only son of a Jewish merchant who was well on his way to prosperity and social respectability.

In 1883, as had happened before and was to happen again, anti-Semitic riots broke out in Prague. Anti-Semitism, the oldest form of collective hatred in Western civilization, had become organized during the last decades of the nineteenth century, and in Prague as elsewhere clerical and nationalist parties kept the hatred against the Jews smouldering. Curses and derisive shouts uttered by Czechs as well as Germans now and then reminded the child, and the man, Kafka that he did not belong.

But Prague harbored other hatreds besides anti-Semitism. About 1900 it had roughly 415,000 Czech and 21,000 German-speaking inhabitants, of whom a small majority, about 11,000, were Jews. The German-Austrians were the socially important and wealthy masters of Czech servants, maids, clerks, and other lowly employees whom they despised. The Czechs answered contempt with an ancient national hatred against the Germans, their oppressors, which was intensified by class hatred.

As in his home town so in his home, the mood of oppression surrounded Kafka. His father Herrmann had worked his way up from being a despised Jew who peddled notions to become the respected owner of a wholesale business in fancygoods. Herrmann Kafka's father, a second son, did not acquire the right to marry until 1848 when this privilege was first extended to all sons by the new constitution. He was then thirty-five

17

years old, a poor country butcher; and Herrmann, his son, had
to work hard and suffer many privations as a child. Talking to
Franz and his sisters about those days, he would shame them
by stressing how ignorant they were of real poverty and hard
work. His rise to prosperity and the upper middle class had
convinced him that there hardly existed goals in life other
than financial and social success, and that no opinions were
valid except his own, since success had proven him right in
everything. Even in the patriarchal German Jewish family
circles of his day he was considered a tyrant.

Trying to mediate between her husband and her children
was his wife, Julie née Löwy, who came, on her mother's side,
from a family with a tradition of producing rabbis, scholars,
and physicians. One of her brothers, Dr. Siegfried Löwy, was
Kafka's favorite uncle. In the Moravian village, where he was
a country doctor, his nephew frequently spent his vacations
and later recuperated from academic cares in the rustic surroundings, a welcome guest in the home of the perennial
bachelor. Two other brothers of his mother only stimulated
young Kafka's imagination. They both had emigrated, Alfred
Löwy, likewise a bachelor, to Madrid, where he was chief
director of the Spanish railroads, and Josef to the Congo, where
he founded a large colonial company.

Having to help her husband in the store, Mrs. Kafka did not
have much time for Franz. When the boy was six, the oldest
of her three daughters, who absorbed the mother's free time
in later years, was born. In this setting, the father, a born
business man, for many years vainly tried to remake his son, a
born writer, in his own image. The story of their unequal
struggle was later told by the son in a letter which, due to its
length (sixty-one printed pages), its pathetic content, and its
style has become a curious masterpiece of German literature.
In this letter, the thirty-seven-year-old son settles with his sixty-
seven-year-old father, making an overpowering case against
paternal absolutism; an ex-slave accusing a tyrant whose power
is waning, a broken son defending himself against a sorrowing
father. Fortunately, the letter never reached the addressee. As
so often, the mother protected her beloved husband from a
fruitless interruption of his routine.

Kafka saw in his father a "gigantic man" and a "court of
final appeal." What gave this man such superiority that even
his grown son, loved and admired by many, felt like nothing
before him? Kafka lists "Physical strength, health, appetite, robust
voice, rhetorical talent, self-contentedness, superiority as a man
of the world, endurance, presence of mind, knowledge of his
fellow men, the capacity of doing things in a grand style,"[1] all
qualities he did not possess. But then the letter continues by
enumerating the corresponding flaws and weaknesses into which
the father is whipped from time to time by his violent temper.

Not afraid of corporal punishment, but in continuous fear
of his father's frequent and loudly voiced disapproval of all he
was and did, the frail, dreamy child spent an unhappy youth.
In vain did his father tell him that only with such masculine
qualities as hardness and aggressiveness had he succeeded in
his fight against a hostile world. For many years Franz Kafka
did not forgive his father for his stubborn and exclusive respect
for the laws by which he lived, and his contempt for his
son's feelings.

Although Herrmann Kafka had known what it meant to be
a lowly Jew whom people sometimes would not let into their
houses, he had not learned compassion for those who were
weaker than he. He was probably harder and more contemptuous toward his Czech employees than most other shopowners
of the German enclave. His son remembered with horror: "You
I heard and saw shouting, cursing and raging in the shop, in
a way that in my opinion at that time had not its equal any-
where in the world." He remembers his father's often repeated
wish that a tubercular clerk should "croak." He reminds him
how he used to talk of his employees as "paid enemies," and
adds accusingly in the *Letter*, "and that was what they were
too, but even before they became such you seemed to me to
be their 'paying enemy.' "[2]

Kafka's early developed sensitivity about injustice drove him
to take the side of the Czech people, and to become interested
in their political problems, their literature, and their language,
which he spoke fluently. This close contact with the Czechs
was one way in which the rebellious young Germans in Prague
revolted against their elders. Of the famous writers who were

more or less Kafka's Prague contemporaries only Franz Werfel knew no Czech. The poet Rainer Maria Rilke learned it against the will of his mother, who, like most Germans of that older generation, despised the "language of the servants." Kafka's youngest sister, Ottla, joining her brother in his revolt against the father and the mores of his generation, often angered the old Kafka by sitting in the kitchen talking Czech with the maid.

Witnessing the unjust treatment of the Czech employees in his father's store seems to have considerably strengthened the gentle boy's aversion to prejudices, and to have helped him to acquire the characteristic which all who came in contact with him sensed: his *Güte*. This German word designates more than its English dictionary equivalent, "kindness"; it is a kindness which has stood the test of having come in contact with man's brutality, his viciousness, and his indifference to his fellow men's suffering.

This sophisticated and strong kindness became the distinguishing feature of Kafka's character; it seems to live in the melancholy smile of his pictures, but Kafka criticism induced those responsible for the photographic Kafka image to change his facial expressions. The photograph chosen to appear in books, magazines, newspaper articles, encyclopedias, and on blurbs is the one taken shortly before his death, and ever since the 1950s even that picture of the moribund sufferer has been retouched until the last remnant of a faint smile has disappeared and the melancholy quester has been changed into a cadaverous-looking zealot with burning eyes, a Prague Savonarola.

In spite of his kindness, Kafka was not an easy man to live with, as his close friends and, above all, he himself knew well. In his frequent self-characterizations, he singled out what he considered to be his negative qualities. There appear, in the first place, weakness, lack of self-confidence, and his inability to act without examining the possible consequences beforehand, "a typical vice of officials" as he calls it, although, in his case, it seems to have been less a professional disease than the result of his education.

Nevertheless, Kafka remained attached to the home that had done such serious damage to him. His indecision and lack of confidence made it impossible for him to leave the power sphere of his father and "little mother Prague." When finally, in 1923, strengthened by a loving woman, he separated from his home and hometown, it was too late, for he had less than a year to live. Besides the *Ausweglosigkeit*, the no exit situation, which originated at home, there was the absence of a law by which Kafka could live, which plagued him all his life. He blamed his home for not having given him a sense of security through the law of Judaism. To his father, Judaism was the fulfillment of certain social obligations; he honored a handful of Jewish customs and paid the synagogue about four visits a year. What these visits meant to little Franz the *Letter* also reveals: "And so I yawned and dozed through the many hours. (I don't think I was ever again so bored except later at dancing lessons.)"[3] Old Herrmann Kafka's faith is shortly defined: "At bottom the faith that ruled your life consisted in your believing in the unconditional rightness of the opinions prevailing in a particular class of Jewish society."[4]

The father was not the only person to be feared. The second torturer in Kafka's childhood was the cook, whom he mentions more than twenty years later, in his diary, as one of his "educators" who had done him harm. She was a harsh, elderly woman who saw to it that the severe, repressive education of the father was continued in his absence. One of her functions was to take the six-year-old boy to the German elementary school, "a place of horror in itself," which she made even more horrible for about a year. When leaving the house, the cook told little Franz that she would tell the teacher how naughty he had been at home. Pleading frantically and struggling in vain to stop until she had forgiven him, the boy was dragged to school. The cook said nothing, but Franz realized that there was always the possibility that she might do so the next time.

The above descriptions are taken from Kafka's letter to a woman friend, Milena, written more than thirty years after these events, and they are one of the indications that his unpleasant childhood experiences were traumatic shocks never to be forgotten.

The ominous walk to school held, however, even more horrors for the nervous child, who had to walk through the Meat-Market-Street across the Meat Market to his school, whose full name was "Elementary School at the Meat Market." Every schoolday for four years the sensitive boy had to pass sights quite different from those which modern meat stores offer. There were gutted pigs and halved oxen hanging from meat hooks, and on platters in the store windows lay pigsheads in pools of blood.

These impressions reappear in Kafka's works and diaries, where he often writes about executioners, butcher knives, stabbings, piles of meat, and the devouring of meat. In 1913, for example, he wrote in his diary: "Always the image of a butcher's broad knife that quickly and with mechanical regularity chops into me from the side and cuts off very thin slices which fly off almost like shavings because of the speed of the action."[5]

In 1892 Kafka exchanged the sober schoolhouse at the sinister Meat Market for the Kinsky palace, one of the fine seventeenth-century buildings of Prague which once belonged to Bohemian aristocracy. The second floor of this baroque structure now housed the humanistic secondary school, called *Deutsches Gymnasium,* which had thus found a fitting exterior for its honorably antiquated spirit of classicism and humanism.

The generous pension laws attracted ungifted teachers; but how could even a good teacher have succeeded in arousing the interest of these adolescents in the humanistic ideals of Thucydides or Cicero vitiated, as they were, by parents, church, and the spirit of the industrial age with its predominantly commercial concerns! A true humanist would have to be a lover of truth and beauty, a man of urbanity and poise whose training in critical thinking should enable him to see the flaws in the arguments proffered by political, national, and religious zealots. But such men were not even called for at the beginning of the twentieth century, which was to become a century of world wars and violent revolutions. Besides, Kafka was enough of a Jew to sense the additional conflict between his cultural traditions and the spirit of humanism.

In 1901 Kafka passed the *Abitur* ("graduation examination") which he and many fellow sufferers had anticipated through years of frightful worrying. Old Kafka allowed his son to recuperate on the North Sea islands of Norderney and Helgoland, where the first great German Jewish poet, Heinrich Heine, had recovered from similar stresses. Unlike Heine, Kafka was

never inspired to write about the sea or other grandiose mani-
festations of nature with which he was familiar. The scene of
his writings is usually Prague, not as a visual image, but as
an atmosphere mixed with that of the old Jewish ghetto which
he knew, not from firsthand experience, but as a region of the
soul: "We walk through the broad streets of the newly built
town. But our steps and our glances are uncertain. Inside we
tremble just as before in the ancient streets of our misery.
Our heart knows nothing of the slum clearance which has been
achieved. The unhealthy old Jewish town within us is far more
real than the new hygienic town around us. With our eyes
open we walk through a dream: ourselves only a ghost of a
vanished age."[6]

Not "a ghost of a vanished age," but quite alive were the
objections against Jews in old Austria. Pressured by his father,
relatives, and friends, Kafka "chose," after a short excursion
into the field of German literature, the study of law. The most
famous German writers who had been law students were Goethe
and Heine, and although the latter also lamented about his
enforced study, he does not seem to have been as unhappy a
law student as Kafka, who writes as follows about the pains
the cramming sessions caused him, using his favorite figure of
speech, a food metaphor: "So I studied Law. This meant that
in the few months before the exams ... I was positively living,
in an intellectual sense, on saw dust, which had, moreover,
already been chewed for me in thousands of other people's
mouths."[7]

His Alma Mater, the Karolo-Ferdinandea in Prague, was a
depressing place. Historical necessity and the mutual hatred
of Czechs and Germans had split it into a German and Czech
university. Kafka, of course, was drilled in the German part
from 1901 to 1906. During his years of study, the relations
between the Czechs and Germans worsened. Students at the
Prague university did not experience the youthful, carefree
atmosphere so often encountered at German and Austrian universities at that time. The German university of Prague was
doomed, and the end cast its shadow ahead. That end came
officially on October 18, 1945, when the president of the Czech
republic decreed that "the German University of Prague which

ceased to exist on May 5, 1945 ... shall, as an institution hostile
to the Czech people, be dissolved forever."[8]

II *Various Teachers*

The doctor's degree, acquired in 1906, followed its bearer for
a while beyond the grave. In the early seventies, the first tree
at the entrance of a melancholy alley in the Prague Jewish ceme-
tery still bore a sign with an arrow and the inscription "Dr.
Franz Kafka," guiding to his grave all those not forbidden by
their government to read the works of this "bourgeois defeatist."

The academic title meant an end to long years of drill, but
not to extracurricular studies begun at the *Gymnasium.* Already
at the age of fifteen, Kafka had been drawn into the struggle
concerning contradictory explanations of God, man, the state,
and nature which had reached a climax in the second half of
the nineteenth century. Kafka began his quest embracing two
"main errors of the time" as pointed out by the papal encyclical
of 1864: pantheism and naturalism. According to the report
of one of his classmates, he wanted to convert the young man
to Spinoza's pantheism but abandoned this doctrine when inspired by a teacher who was an enthusiastic evolutionist. With
a small group of like-minded classmates, Kafka now studied
Darwin and, with particular enthusiasm, his German apostle
Haeckel, both banned from school libraries.

The shock administered by Darwin's book *The Descent of
Man* (1871) had not yet worn off when the Germans received
an even severer shock in *Die Welträtsel* (The Mysteries of the
World) by Dr.Phil., Dr.Med., Dr.Jur., Dr.Scient. Ernst Haeckel,
professor of zoology at the University of Jena. This modern
Dr. Faustus presented, in a learned yet intelligible style, his
own monistic philosophy which, he claimed, was the philosophy
of the future. As one of the *terribles simplificateurs* among
scientists at the end of the nineteenth century he wrote: "The
great abstract law of mechanical causality ... rules now the
universe as well as the human spirit; it is the secure immovable
lodestar," and so on.[9] Its rule did not last long, but while it
lasted it made the believers happy, proud, and overbearing.

Much as Kafka admired the thoughts of Haeckel even at

that time, he did not believe in messianic solutions but kept on looking for masters from whom counsel might be obtained. When he was about sixteen years old, he was introduced to Nietzsche by his former classmate and close friend Oskar Pollak. Subsequently, he studied the controversial philosopher's *Thus Spoke Zarathustra*, but later came to dislike this work, probably because of the fanatic self-assurance and the exuberant style in which the ailing prophet presented it.

Kafka's lifelong admiration belonged to Goethe whom he studied with particular zest in 1912, the year in which he and Brod made a pilgrimage to Weimar, where Goethe had spent almost fifty-seven of his eighty-two years. The January 24, 1912 diary entry reports the "greed," "thoroughness," and "joy" with which Kafka read a 500-page French book on German Jewish literature, and on the fourth of the following month he makes a similarly jubilant statement about the zeal with which he reads Goethe, "permeating every part of me, . . . keeping me from all writing."[10] It must be remembered that not to write when he had the urge to was the greatest sacrifice Kafka could make.

A German author, Walter Jens, has praised Kafka's preference for the world of the Eastern Jews, in their strength always renewing themselves from within, over the undecided Western Jews, because he had "the insight that the filth of the ghetto still hides infinitely greater wonders, legends, and mysteries than the hygienic world of Goethe-reading Western Jews."[11] The author of this hyperbole forgot that the hygienically living Kafka, being more than a Goethe reader, was a Goethe admirer. Jens stresses the contrast between Goethe and Judaism, but it was exactly with this contrast that Kafka lived all his life without ever letting it turn into a conflict.

Of course, there were also many affinities between the two writers. Apart from epitomizing excellence in prose, Goethe inspired Kafka with his faith that love and organic growth, not hatred and volcanic eruption, can create a better world for man. When his future fiancée, Felice Bauer, asked him to recommend a book to her, Kafka told her to read Goethe's *The Sorrows of Young Werther*. The choice shows his superior insight as a critic; to his contemporaries, this novel was no more than a sentimental love story, while actually it spoke eloquently of their own sorrows too. The early twentieth century was just as much a declining age as the eighteenth in its second half, those prerevolutionary years when Werther suffered because of the falsification of values and the lessening of the quality of life.

It may be assumed that Felice never realized the similarity between Werther and Kafka to which her fiancé might have wanted to draw her attention. Both are sensitive to the lot of all those who are oppressed, unhappy, frustrated. They both suffer, Werther because of the vicious class discrimination of his day, Kafka because of racial discrimination. "The insolence of office" that causes Werther to give up working for a livelihood is, in Kafka's case, the burden of office which he did not dare to drop. Werther seldom writes to his widowed mother, whose sense of values he despises; Kafka was barely speaking with his father, and only a little more with his mother, for the same reasons. The unhappiness of the fictitious and the real lover had different causes, but neither man had the strength to end the hopeless struggle for the loved woman. Both use the image of being incarcerated for their feeling of being frustrated in the world, and both seek the same "way out," a favorite metaphor of Kafka, through war or suicide—Kafka, of course, only in his diary and letters.

In one regard, Kafka was even unhappier than Werther. The unfortunate young man of the late eighteenth century had found, with Rousseau's help, the new law in a declining age: "nature" and "the natural." Goethe had found a law more acceptable than that of his unhappy hero in the life-style of the aristocratic Weimar Court, to which he could add, without conflict, the ideals of the classical world: poise, dignity, respect, beauty. Subsequent writers had to live with the shallow life-style, or the lack thereof, prevailing in the rapidly developing industrial nations of the nineteenth century. One of the great writers who suffered painfully from the necessity of living in such a time was Gustave Flaubert. After, or together with, Goethe, it was he whom Kafka most admired and whom he studied, paying close attention to his style, reading his works in the original French.

Kafka sent Felice Bauer Flaubert's novel *L'Education senti-*

mentale and confessed in the accompanying letter: "But *Education sentimentale* . . . is a book that for many years has been as
dear to me as are only two or three people; whenever or wherever I opened it, I am startled and succumb to it completely,
and I always feel as though I were the author's spiritual son,
albeit a weak and awkward one."[12] Kafka could identify himself
with Flaubert, the man who had also been an unwilling law
student, knew severe illness, and led a solitary life solely dedicated to writing. Flaubert, the novelist, probably taught him
more than other writers to choose comparatively insignificant
heroes and to show them in action, without displaying the narrator's feelings, with complete *impassibilité* ("detachment").

In her *Souvenirs intimes*, Flaubert's niece recounts how, accompanied by her uncle, she had visited a friend, a charming
young woman playing happily with her lovely, healthy children.
Deeply moved, Flaubert said repeatedly on their way home:
"Ils sont dans le vrai" ("They live in the truth"). Kafka loved
that phrase and, according to Brod, quoted it often. One such
quotation, slightly altered, is included in one of his letters to
Felice in which he discusses the misunderstanding between them:
"We must start afresh. That We, however, does not refer to
you, for you were and are in the right (*im Richtigen*). . . ."[13]

Far removed from Goethe and Flaubert was another "teacher,"
Jizschak Löwy, the star performer of the Polish Yiddish company which performed in a shabby restaurant in Prague from
October, 1911, to January, 1912. The actors, above all Löwy,
and most of the plays were a profound experience for Kafka.
Never did he express in his diaries greater admiration for any
contemporary than he does in the entry of October, 1911: "At
the end of the performance we [Kafka and his friend Max Brod]
still expect the actor Löwy, whom I would admire in the dust."[14]
With the seeming hyperbole Kafka eulogized the man Löwy
more than the actor. He admired this young man who, in spite
of strong inner resistance, had disregarded the objections of his
Chassidic parents, to whom the theater was *trefe* ("ritually
unclean"). He admired the cultural messenger from the East
who so ably reminded him and the other Westernized Jews in
the audience of their common cultural heritage. And yet, for
Löwy and the other Yiddish actors life was pitiful. As Eastern

Jews they were despised and ridiculed even by many Western
Jews. Sixteen years after his friendship with Löwy began, Kafka
still reproached his father for having forbidden him to bring
Löwy into the house because, as he told his son: "he who goes
to bed with dogs gets up with fleas."

Not being able to receive his friend at home, Kafka took
long walks with him and listened eagerly as the young pariah,
accepting the insult with equanimity, told him about the Talmud
and the Zohar (the holiest mystical book of the kabala), his
Chassidic parents, his own hard life in Poland and abroad, about
Yiddish and Hebrew literature, and again and again about the
great plays of the Yiddish theater. In his autobiography, Brod
speaks of the "wretched troupe of Eastern Jewish actors . . . a
true image of Jewry, frightfully repelling, but also with magic
attraction, taking on a meaning which was deepened for both
of us through Kafka's enthusiasm."[15]

After this breakthrough Kafka remained aware that he was
a Jew, and, although never a true believer, he was, all his life,
concerned with important aspects of Judaism. The idea of
going to Palestine became, in his last years, his life's deepest
wish. But long before that time he had begun to study Hebrew
with an intensity not explained by any plans of emigration,
which would have been very vague in 1918. Brod reports in
his Kafka biography that at that time his friend called Hebrew
and horticulture the "positive" and the "rustic" elements in
his life.[16]

It seems ridiculous to mention, after Goethe, Flaubert, and
Löwy, nature-cure practitioners as influential teachers of Kafka;
but he was their enthusiastic disciple, believing in their theories
until his death, which was probably hastened by his fanatic
belief in them. Besides spending much vacation time in their
health camps, he studied their publications, sought their advice
and followed it, living a strictly vegetarian existence, sleeping
even in winter with the window open, and always wearing light
clothing. Especially dangerous for his own health was his blind
acceptance of the warnings of nature healers against medical
doctors, medicines, vaccinations, and injections. His unshakable
belief in the malpractice of medical doctors drove him all his
life to violent outbursts against them. He calls every internist

"a gentleman who deserves to be shot."[17] Sanatoria for the tubercular, which he had to visit during his fatal illness, he calls places "where one has to eat meat, where ex-hangmen dislocate one's arms if one resists the injections, and where beard-stroking Jewish doctors, as callous toward Jew as Christian, look on."[18] How devoted he was to the dogmas of the nature-cure practitioners is expressed most earnestly in the novel fragment *Die erste lange Eisenbahnfahrt* (*The First Long Journey by Train*), ". . . If I am not right in this matter [nature cures] I am wrong in everything."[19]

CHAPTER 2

Incongruities

I *Two Desks*

THE years of drilling had finally earned Kafka the position of an Austrian official. His father deserves credit for not having urged his son at an early stage to enter a business career. He respected the "loftier ideas," that is, his son's mentality which was so different from his own, but the son quite wrongly contradicted him: "They [the loftier ideas] would have had to express themselves differently, instead of letting me float quickly and timidly through my schooling and my law studies until finally I landed up at a clerk's desk."[1] But he landed for good at the writer's desk, no matter how disturbing and harmful to his creative impulses the servitude at the other desk was.

Kafka also exaggerated when he told his father that "he floated timidly" to the official's desk. He certainly showed no timidity during the last stretch of that swim which was strenuous to the end. Before passing his doctoral examinations, he had to acquire a year's legal experience as a precondition for entering government service; and so he served part of that time at the criminal court of Prague. That choice was not necessary and certainly shows no timidity on his part; it was perhaps prompted by an inner need to experience the world of crime and punishment which was later to appear in two of his prominent works.

After the drab labor of the last years of preparation, and before and during the first months at the detested office desk, exotic wishes flared up in Kafka which never completely subsided. Exotism in literature and life is the yearning to escape, even if only in one's imagination, to the Orient or a tropical country where passions are believed to be stronger and where fauna, flora, and climate are more exciting than in Europe. Its

the company: "Dr. Kafka is an eminently diligent worker, enormously gifted and devoted to his duties."[9] His colleagues, especially those below him, praised his humaneness and tact, and stated that he had not a single enemy in the company. In the almost fourteen years during which his health allowed him to work there, he rose quickly to the highest position accessible to him.

After a look at the official Kafka as the insurance company saw him, it is astounding to see the entirely different picture Kafka presents of himself as an official in his letters and diaries. After less than three years in the Workers' Accident Company he wrote to Pfohl, who had become a father substitute to his lonely employee: "... I am completely overworked, not by the office, but by my other work. ... It is a horrible double life, from which there is probably no escape but insanity."[10]

In December, 1912, Kafka told Felice in a lighter vein what the work at the writer's desk, on which lay the unfinished story "Metamorphosis," had done to his office desk. "My desk at the office was certainly never tidy, but now it is littered with a chaotic pile of papers and files; I may just know the things that lie on top, but lower down I suspect nothing but horrors."[11]

The situation did not improve. In 1921 Kafka said bitterly to Janouch: "The Institution is a dark nest of bureaucrats, in which I function as the solitary display-Jew."[12] About the same time he argues in his diary:

I am wrong when I complain that I have never been caught up in the current of life, that I never made my escape from Prague, was never made to learn a sport or trade, and so forth—I should probably have refused every offer. ... I allowed only incongruous things to claim my attention, my law studies, the job at the office. ...[13]

These are the last remarks which that Austrian official entered into his diary about his unloved work before his illness forced him to give it up.

II *The Phantom Woman*

The thirty-one-year-old bachelor Kafka had worked for five years at his official's desk when he began to wage the hardest struggle of his life, the struggle against a threatening marriage. On August 13, 1912, he had accidentally met Felice Bauer at the home of Brod's parents. A month and a half later he described his first impressions of her in his diary:

... although she was sitting at the table, she struck me as a maid-servant. ... Bony, empty face that wore its emptiness openly. ... Almost broken nose. Blond, somewhat straight, unattractive hair, strong chin. As I was taking my seat I looked at her closely for the first time, by the time I was seated I already had an unchangeable opinion.[14]

The words "unchangeable opinion," so unfitting for an incipient love, appear at the beginning of the relationship like an omen portending struggles, accusations, mediations, the whole sometimes resembling a legal brief.

Five weeks after he had met her, he wrote his first letter to Miss Bauer, starting an epistolary love affair which was destined to last, despite several interruptions, for more than five years of sorrow, self-accusations, even despair on Kafka's side, and almost continuous attempts on her side to understand the fascinating but difficult genius, as Brod, one of the mediators between the two, had implored her to do. The letters Kafka wrote to Felice between September 20 and December 21, 1912, account for 182 pages of the closely printed 700-page edition of his letters to her, which appeared in 1967, seven years after Felice had died in her American home.

It soon became clear to Kafka that Felice had a mind of her own; she was not the usual middle-class girl trained to submit to her future master. Although she lived with her parents, she worked for a Berlin manufacturer of gramophones and dictaphones, and had risen, in three years, from typist to clerk. Her character and her practical talents, her unusual abilities to fight life's battle, won Kafka's lifelong admiration: whether he really loved her in the ordinary sense of the word must be doubted, as Felice came to doubt it despite the fervor and frequency of his letters.

Kafka wrote two, sometimes three, letters a day and begged continuously for prompt answers; but in the midst of all the restrained passion and unrestrained longing there appears early, that is, in the second month of their correspondence, an ominous tone, an excuse for having to write shorter letters from now on: "Because I want to spend every ounce of myself on my novel [*Amerika*], which after all belongs to you as well, or rather it should give you a clearer idea of the good in me than the mere hints in the longest letters of the longest lifetime."[15]

Sixteen days and thirty-one letters after this warning, after the "dearest lady" address had changed to "dearest," Kafka, the lawyer, helped the lover Kafka to convince Felice that the inspired author Kafka could not use the five free days he had at Christmas time to visit her, implying that it would be spiritual murder to ask him to do so. She was convinced, and he did not see her until March.

Kafka spent six days of June, 1913, composing a letter, five pages in print, in which he asked her to marry him, at the same time belittling himself with the weirdest hyperboles: "...I am unable to reason.... Nor can I tell a story properly; in fact I can hardly even talk...."[16] It is understandable that Felice asked him, in one of her last letters, whether he had always been truthful with her, and he gave her, as so often, a vague answer which was no more than a diplomatically veiled "no."

But that happened four years later. Felice accepted the engagement, and Kafka, obviously worried, implored her in the next letter to think the matter over. He warned her of his need to use the time of the day in a way he has found most favorable for his writing: "But what, dearest Felice, have you to say to the kind of married life in which the husband, at any rate for several months in the year, returns from the office at 2:30 or 3, eats, lies down, sleeps until 7 or 8, hurriedly has his supper, takes an hour's walk, and then starts writing, and writes till 1 or 2? Could you really stand that?"[17] He further warns her that he does not want to see anyone in his home, and, of course, he still avoids seeing her.

Three of these letters are most indicative of the continuous indecision with which Kafka tortured himself and Felice. Two months after he had proposed to her, she vacationed on the island of Sylt, in the North Sea. In his first letter to Sylt he wrote of the "splendid idea" that she, without losing a part of the vacation time, should return to Berlin by way of Prague.

Did he not realize that this trip (on the map a slightly curved line Sylt–Berlin–Prague) meant a detour of many train hours? Did he really believe that limiting her stay to only a few more hours in Prague would not make any difference as far as her vacation time was concerned? Considering his lack of practical sense, one must assume that he really thought so.

What Kafka did not believe for long was that his idea was so splendid. On the following day he retracted his suggestion: "I dream about you almost every night, such is my need to be near you. But, for a multitude of reasons, my fear is just as great. I don't think I shall come to Berlin at all while we are engaged, even if we were not to get married until May. Would this be all right for you, and particularly for the others? Can you agree to it?"[18]

On the third day he reversed his position again. What makes this letter so important is that Kafka reveals for the first time whom he really loves.

Dearest Felice, I withdraw everything I may have said yesterday. The apprehension that keeps me from you at present, that also prevents me from wishing you were coming to Prague, is justified; but there is still greater justification for my immense apprehension, far surpassing the other, that I shall perish if we are not together soon. For if we are not together soon, my love for you, which refuses any other thought to enter my head, would be directed toward an imaginary idea, toward a phantom, toward something totally un- attainable and at the same time and at all times indispensable; but if this were so it might be enough to rip me out of this world. I tremble as I write. So come, Felice, come to Prague if you possibly can on your return journey.[19]

Felice did not come to Prague. She knew the risk that he might "perish" was small; she had read by now too many hyperboles and seven descriptions of suicidal moods.

To the detriment of both herself and her fiancé-to-be she did not pay attention to the most revealing lines Kafka ever wrote to her, that she was "a phantom." Of course, he was speaking of a future danger, but it had been reality from the very beginning, as she would have noticed had she examined his previous letters with that warning in mind. Later, in 1916,

Kafka admitted to Brod: "I certainly did not know her at all. Apart from other considerations, I was prevented from knowing her because I was downright afraid of the reality of that woman who wrote letters...."[20] The "unattainable yet indispensable" phantom woman was Kafka's Dulcinea, in whom this lonely knight of the spirit believed while he tried with feeble hope to lift the world about which he wrote to the plane of "the pure, the true, the unchangeable."

Gradually Kafka's letters to Felice lost their exalted tone. He himself suggested not writing for a while. During this interim period he had a vacation love affair with an eighteen-year-old-girl in Riva, Italy. "We meant so much to each other," he confessed a little later to his fiancée-to-be.

When he visited Felice in Berlin a month after this confession, he was naively surprised to see how cool she had become toward him. She admitted that she no longer cared to marry him, and among the reasons for this decision she mentioned the loss of good seats in the theater.

At this nadir, a mediator appeared, Grete Bloch, a good friend of Felice, living in Vienna. In his letters, Kafka soon began courting her diplomatically, but unmistakably, while she, disregarding his suggestions of letting friendship slip into love, made him jealous. Despite this diversion, Felice's refusal to marry him had the usual effect. Although he was flirting with Grete Bloch and in spite of Felice's cold, sometimes humiliating behavior, Kafka's eagerness, if not passion, was spurred on, and at a meeting in Berlin, at Easter time, they became informally engaged.

The event did not decrease the tenderness toward Grete Bloch in Kafka's letters, but the "nestbuilding" of Felice made him increasingly irascible. He mocked her in nervous anger: "By the way, don't forget! the thing that plays a far greater part in your trousseau than either furniture or linen is swimming. You promised to report any progress you made."[21]

The official engagement on June 1 was a sad affair for him as well as for Felice; it dampened even his correspondence with Grete, which soon reached its end.[22] In a masterful sentence, sustained in its length of nine printed lines by variegated complex attributes, Kafka explains himself to her as an asocial type:

Ein durch seine Lebensumstände und durch seine Natur gänzlich
unsocialer Mensch, mit nicht festem augenblicklich schwer zu
beurteilendem Gesundheitszustand, durch sein nichtzionistisches (ich
bewundere den Zionismus und ekle mich vor ihm) und nichtgläubiges
Judentum von jeder grossen, tragenden Gemeinschaft ausgeschieden,
durch die Zwangsarbeit des Bureaus in seinem besten Wesen unauf-
hörlich auf das quälendste erschüttert—ein solcher Mensch entschliesst
sich, allerdings unter dem stärksten innersten Zwang, zum Heiraten,
also zur socialsten Tat. Das scheint mir nicht wenig für einen
solchen Menschen.[23]

Owing to circumstances as well as to his own temperament, a completely antisocial man in an indifferent state of health hard to
determine at the moment, excluded from every great soul-sustaining
community on account of his non-Zionist (I admire Zionism and am
nauseated by it), nonpracticing Judaism; the most precious part of
his nature continually and most agonizingly upset by the enforced
labor of his office—a man of this kind, certainly under the deepest
inner compulsion, decides to get married—to undertake, in other
words, the most social of acts. For a man of this kind, that strikes
me as no mean venture.

It was too much of a venture. On July 12 the engagement was
broken off in Berlin.

Immediately after that defeat, Kafka went on a vacation to
the Baltic Sea, but the stupor that possessed him remained
until, traveling home by train, he was shaken out of it. He
saw in his compartment a girl who reminded him of G.W., the
girl in Riva. His confession that she had meant much to him
had started Felice's alienation from him, now the memory of
G.W. makes his dulled feelings stir. This otherwise unattractive
girl on the train had "sparkling, inextinguishable eyes." G.W. had
fascinated him two years ago with a glance he never forgot,
and which he described: "Too late. The sweetness of sorrow and
of love. To be smiled at by her in the boat. That was the most
beautiful of all. Always only the desire to die and the not-yet-
yielding, this alone is love."[24] Never again seems love to have
enchanted Kafka-Tristan as here on an Italian lake where he
found it in the smile of an eighteen-year-old girl.

Half a year after the disengagement, Felice wrote again, Kafka
answering immediately, and in January, 1915, they met in Boden-

bach, a Bohemian bordertown. His detailed description of this desolate meeting touches upon the main difficulties which, in the end, prevented the marriage: her lack of erotic appeal, disinterest in his literary work, unwillingness to respect his "phantastic" life, as he calls it, made necessary by his literary work and the rules imposed by the nature-cure practitioners upon their disciples.

Felice could not be his Isolde. Her love was not close to death, but part of life, a life as envisaged by millions of "normal" girls of her class: a family housed among the furniture in the heavy style of the day, which Kafka detested.

Despite the failure of their encounter in Bodenbach, Kafka and Felice risked another meeting a year and a half later, this time in Marienbad, where they lived in adjoining rooms for ten days in July, 1916. At first it seemed to become the worst experience for both in this unhappy affair, but a few days later an uncommon tone appears in the diary: "With F. I was intimate only in letters, as a human being not until two days ago. Not everything clears up in spite of that, doubts remain, but wonderful is the stilled glance of her eyes, the opening up of womanly depth."[25]

Their relationship after Marienbad seemed improved. In September Felice, at the advice of her fiancé, had joined a Home for Jewish People as an assistant teacher of young girls, refugees from Polish Galicia. Kafka helped her with books he sent, and his pedagogical counseling was beyond the insight of his time. The old question, for example, of why foreign languages should be taught, he answers in a truly humanistic sense: "The study of languages can be based on the statement that it constitutes the first practical step of applied love of one's fellow man, which expresses itself in the true realization of inner hospitality, in detachment from the narrowness of one's own feelings, and in entering an alien point of view, thus creating greater tolerance and humility. *Without this experience, merely learning a language achieves but little*" (italics mine).[26]

Here, as everywhere, Kafka is concerned with the values of inner life, without which, in his opinion, nothing valuable in outer life can be achieved. Here lies the reason why he was opposed to those who put their trust in systems, be it language instruction or political activities believed to bring about another golden age.

In spite of the harmony created by their common interest in the Jewish Home, the relationship deteriorated again. In those last years Felice, more concerned than Kafka, visited him in Prague, and they became engaged again at the beginning of July, 1917. But then his body took over. On September 4, tuberculosis in both ends of the lung was diagnosed, the threatening marriage could now be avoided. Unwilling at first to go to a medically supervised sanatorium, Kafka went to Zürau, a village where his sister Ottla administered a small country estate belonging to a brother-in-law. His love for Felice had disappeared; yet she tried desperately, but in vain, to win him back. At the end of September she came to Zürau. His diary entry sums up the sad end: "Felice was here, traveled thirty hours to see me; I should have prevented her. As I see it, she is suffering the utmost misery, and the guilt is essentially mine. I myself am unable to take hold of myself, am as helpless as I am unfeeling. ...I am guilty of the wrong for which she is being tortured, and am in addition the torturer...."[27] The second engagement was broken off at Christmas time in 1917.

On his deathbed Kafka was asked if Felice had understood him, and he wrote on a slip of paper the chivalrous answer: "She did, as far as it was worthwhile understanding me."[28]

CHAPTER 3

Kafka's Style

K AFKA began to write in 1897, but it is difficult to outline
the development of his style since his writings before 1912
are lost, with the exception of some sketches, a larger fragment,
which Brod entitled "Wedding Preparations in the Country,"
and one complete story, "Description of a Struggle." Although
not works of fiction, a few letters he wrote between February,
1902, and January, 1904, may be added to this short list of
works indicative of his early style. The letters were directed
to his former schoolmate and fellow student, Oskar Pollak, a
solitary young man of sharp intellect and a Nietzsche disciple
whose friendship Kafka sought. His letters to Pollak are extraordinary, filled with phantasies, short narratives, aphorisms, and
philosophical reflections, all of which frequently raise them to
the level of literary works.

In 1903 the young law student Kafka promised Pollak to send
him his extant writings, except a few pieces censored by the
author as too personal, and a few *Kindersachen* ("childhood
stuff"). In regard to his childhood efforts he remarked: "You
see this kind of misfortune has been riding me since early
times."[1] Writing to Pollak two months later, he returned to the
idea, but this time masterfully, in aphoristic form: "God does
not want me to write, but I, I must.... But by lamenting one
cannot shake millstones off one's neck, if one loves them."[2] Two
more aphorisms from this early period may be quoted as
examples of his mastery in this genre, as displayed not only
in his diaries, letters, and publications, but also in conversations,
as those who knew Kafka personally report: "Many a book works
like a key to unfamiliar halls in one's own castle,"[3] and "A book
must be the axe for the frozen sea in us."[4]

One of the letters, written shortly before Christmas, 1902,

41

contains a little "Kafkaesque" story, the first of its kind which
is preserved.[5] Two odd characters meet. One is called "the
bashful tall one" and lives in an old village, whereas the other,
"the one dishonest in his heart," lives in a big town "which got
drunk, evening by evening, and raged, evening by evening."
Shortly before Christmas, the tall one is sitting crouched near
the window, letting his legs, which do not fit into the room,
dangle outside the window. "The dishonest one" comes to visit
him, and his words are "distinguished gentlemen with patent
leather shoes and English neckties and shining buttons." The
dishonest one plagues the bashful tall one with his words, which
bite and pinch; and after he has gone, the tall one cries and
wonders whether his God or his devil had sent him the other one.

In this story, tall Kafka humbling himself before small, frail
Pollak has metamorphosed himself into two characters, the
bashful naive side within him represented by the country
bumpkin with the "skeletal legs," and "the dishonest one," who
is the young law student Kafka, the well-dressed big-city
dweller who goes to the races, the cabarets, and the wine
restaurants with their tempting waitresses. Again he humbles
himself before the highly intellectual and sophisticated Pollak
as the country bumpkin, and before Pollak, the Nietzschean
despiser of the big cities and their mentality, as the spurious
man of the world.

Had he said that much in ordinary prose to his friend, he
would have appeared insincere and crawling; but the two characters seem far removed from him, and through his metamorphosed forms he can express without inhibitions what he feels;
even more importantly, he can express what conceptual language
cannot express so well, that is, nuances of feeling, of the emotional atmosphere between him and Pollak. Psychological anal-
ysis would have been too general, would have been boring
and less convincing, which is one reason why Kafka hardly
ever uses this aspect of story telling.

The hero, who usually represents an aspect of Kafka's inner
life, is chiefly one who appears distorted, metamorphosed, ab-
normal or extraordinary in a "normal" world. In his shorter
narratives Kafka's alter ego appears as a snakelike creature:
"Grosser Lärm" ("Much Noise"), a suicide: "Das Urteil" ("The

Judgment"), a beetle: "Die Verwandlung" ("The Metamorphosis"), a chimpanzee: "Ein Bericht für eine Akademie" ("A Report to an Academy"), a trapeze artist: "Erstes Leid" ("First Sorrow"), a hunger artist: "Ein Hungerkünstler" ("A Hunger Artist"), a dog: "Forschungen eines Hundes" ("Investigations of a Dog"), a badger: "Der Bau" ("The Burrow"), or a mouse: "Josefine, die Sängerin" ("Josephine the Singer"). The extraordinary aspects of the heroes in the three novels will be discussed later. Even in his nonliterary statements Kafka speaks occasionally about himself using grotesque distortions, as in an early letter to Brod: ". . . on that day my head was hanging down so heavily that in the evening I noticed with amazement that my chin had grown into my chest. But on the next day I was holding my head nicely up again. . . ."[6] What is distinctly Kafkaesque about such grotesqueries is the absence of any word or phrase to link them, as a comparison or simile, to the rest of the statement. They are, rather, fused with reality, a method which jolts the unsuspecting reader.

Besides such clear indications of his future style, there appear, in the early years, also passages influenced by the contemporary style. Kafka was fully aware of their existence. He wrote to Pollak: "You must keep in mind that I began to write at a time when one 'created works' if one wrote bombast; there is no worse time for a beginner. And I was so crazy about the big words."[7] The literary situation was not to change in his favor. During the more than twenty-five years spanned by his literary career, from the late nineties to the year of his death, 1924, Kafka's contemporaries produced, for the most part, styles alien and even repugnant to him. When he left the *Gymnasium* in 1901, there still prevailed in Germany and Austria voluptuousness with its languor and its melancholy farewells to a by-gone age. When he broke through to his own style in 1912, expressionism, with its apocalyptic despairs and messianic hopes, was beginning to dominate the literary scene. There were outsiders like Thomas Mann, whom Kafka admired, but the masters who influenced his style were men of the past: Heinrich von Kleist, the humble Johann Peter Hebel, Flaubert, and, above all, Goethe.

The style of his closest friend Brod, which was precious and sometimes insincere, never delighted and sometimes even em-

barrassed him. Their differences in literary taste emerged at the
very beginning of their friendship, although Kafka minimized
them. On their first walk together, after a lecture on Nietzsche
given by Brod, Kafka criticized the all too rough formulations
of his new acquaintance, who, among other exaggerations, had
called Nietzsche a "swindler."[8] They then discussed their favorite
authors, and Brod quoted a passage from Gustav Meyrink, falsely
called one of Kafka's forerunners, in which butterflies are compared to "great opened-out books of magic." Kafka disliked this
simile, calling it farfetched and obtrusive. Where he believed he
had discovered insincerity, exaggeration, or artificiality in a literary work, he thought little of the author, even if he ranked high
in the histories of literature, as did Frank Wedekind, Heinrich
Mann, and Oscar Wilde. When his fiancée mentioned Rudolf G.
Binding, then a novice writer who was to be highly respected
in later years, he exploded: I do not know a line of that author
"which is not false, exaggerated, singing."[9]

As Kafka developed his style, he increasingly avoided what
he called "singing," that is, lyrical effusions, rising to rhetorical
heights of enthusiasm or solemnity, fanciful adornments, im-
pressive but incorrect or vague generalizations, without ever
giving up the grotesque element which appears in his earliest
preserved writings.

The following example, taken from *Beschreibung eines Kampfes*
(*Description of a Struggle*) is one of more than twenty phantas-
magorias which, separated by dialogues, spring from a grandiose
imagination playfully delighting in the grotesque. Kafka never
had this work published, but he selected four passages from it
to be included among the sketches and reflections which make
up his first book: *Betrachtung* (Meditation), finished in 1912.
These earliest examples of his published works show a strange
similarity with Rilke's *Die Aufzeichnungen des Malte Laurids
Brigge* (*Notebooks of Malte Laurids Brigge*), a work which set
a new standard in German prose. The following example taken
from Kafka's *Betrachtung*, entitled "Clothes" and written about
1905, and a passage from Rilke's *Malte Laurids Brigge* show
stylistic and topical resemblances all the more surprising since
mutual influence was impossible.

Clothes

Often when I see clothes with manifold pleats, frills, and appendages which fit so smoothly onto lovely bodies I think they won't keep that smoothness long, but will get creases that can't be ironed out, dust lying so thick in the embroidery that it can't be brushed away, and no one would want to be so unhappy and so foolish as to wear the same valuable gown every day from early morning till night.

And yet I see girls who are lovely enough and display attractive muscles and small bones and smooth skin and masses of delicate hair, and nonetheless appear day in, day out, in this same natural fancy dress, always propping the same face on the same palms and letting it be reflected from the looking glass.

Only sometimes at night, on coming home late from a party, it seems in the looking glass to be worn out, puffy, dusty, already seen by too many people, and hardly wearable any longer.[10]

The following observation is made by Rilke's Malte Laurids Brigge, a young Dane who leads a solitary, meditative life in Paris:

To think, for instance, that I have never been aware before how many faces there are. There are quantities of human beings, but there are many more faces, for each person has several. There are people who wear the same face for years; naturally, it wears out, it gets dirty, it splits at the folds, it stretches, like gloves one has worn on a journey. These are thrifty, simple people; they do not change their face, they never even have it cleaned. It is good enough, they say, and who can prove to them the contrary? The question of course arises, since they have several faces, what do they do with the others? They store them up. Their children will wear them. But sometimes, too, it happens that their dogs go out with them. And why not? A face is a face.[11]

Rilke, the great poet and great judge of literature, was one of the first to recognize the greatness of Gide, Proust, Giraudoux, and Kafka. Asking Kafka's publisher to send him everything Kafka might publish he added: "I never read a line this author wrote which did not concern me in a most peculiar way, or amazed me."[12] The older poet discerned stylistic similarities with his own works in the prose writing of his younger Prague fellow citizen, and yet he knew only a few short narratives by Kafka when he wrote to his publisher in 1914.

Approximately seventy-five pages are preserved from whatever

Kafka wrote in the five years following *Beschreibung eines Kampfes* (1905). To this should be added some of his letters and his diary, which he started in 1910.

Throughout Kafka's letters and diaries, there appear sometimes desperate, sometimes jocular, complaints about noises which tortured the nervous author. One source of noise was right at home: an excitable father with a booming voice and three excitable younger sisters, engaged in their domestic activities around his centrally located room, "the passage way between the parents' bedroom and the living room." Kafka's reaction to this noise is first described in a few seminal lines in a letter to Brod, written in December, 1910: "My father is not quite well, he is staying at home. When to the left the breakfast noise stops, the lunchtime noise starts to the right. Now doors are opened everywhere as if the walls were broken open. Above all, however, the center of all misery remains [Kafka in his room]. I cannot write, I have not written a line which I approve of."[13]

In December, 1911, he registers another complaint about his noisy room, this time in his diary: "I want to write with a continuous trembling on my forehead."[14] The second sentence introduces a sketch of twenty-four lines which he published a year later in a German magazine under the title "Much Noise."

I sit in my room in the very headquarters of the uproar of the entire house. I hear all the doors close, because of their noise only the footsteps of those running between them are spared me, I hear even the slamming of the oven door in the kitchen. My father bursts through the doors of my room and passes through in his dragging dressing gown, the ashes are scraped out of the stove in the next room, Valli asks, shouting word for word through the anteroom whether Father's hat has been brushed yet, a hushing that claims to be friendly to me raises the shout of an answering voice. The house door is unlatched and screeches as though from a catarrhal throat, then opens wider with the brief singing of a woman's voice and closes with a dull manly jerk that sounds most inconsiderate. My father is gone, now begins the more delicate, more distracted, more hopeless noise led by the voices of the two canaries. I had already thought of it before, but with the canaries it comes back to me again, that I might open the door a narrow crack, crawl into the next room like a snake and in that way, on the floor, beg my sisters and their governess for quiet.

In the published version, small but significant changes were made by Kafka, by now the mature stylist.

Diary	*Published Version*[15]
Vally asks into indefinite space shouting through the anteroom as through a Parisian (small) street whether father's hat has been brushed yet.	Vally asks, shouting word for word through the anteroom, whether father's hat has been brushed yet.

The direction of the shout "into indefinite space" weakens the impression of its loudness by introducing a visual aspect, and the following simile no longer refers to indefinite space. Vally shouts a question, but in a Parisian street we expect the announcements of a street vendor or the shrill imperative of a housewife. Questions are not the typical street noise. By omitting description (indefinite space) and rhetorical ornament (the comparison) Kafka increases the loudness of Vally's shout, which is also an indirect homage to the all-important father. Vally is the temporary, but intense, supervisor of those preparing the exit of the mighty one.

The simplicity of Kafka's prose is deceptive since it is rich in allusions which stay, however, within the "field" of the story's meaning and require slow and careful reading to be perceived and appreciated in their subtlety; they are not roadsigns pointing to theological heavens or existential hells. Short as "Much Noise" is, stylistically and topically it introduces the series of narratives which begin in 1912.

The sketch begins with a self-ironization so typical of Kafka. He, the helpless sufferer, the weakest member of the entire family, sits in the headquarters of the noise, as if he were the general to whom all the noises have to report. The family's agitation, causing the additional noises which accompany the father's departure, bear loud testimony to the superiority and patriarchal position of the real master. There are noises and sights which suggest symbols of superior power. His crashing through the door calls to mind a wild bull, his moving through the room with trailing dressing gown a warship leaving a trail of smoke as it moves full steam ahead; but, such is Kafka's irony that the trailing bourgeois garment may also nullify the heroic

associations of wild bull and warship. This taking back, this only
apparent self-contradiction, is a stylistic element frequently found
in Kafka's writings, cautioning the reader against the deceptive-
ness of the world of appearances.

Now only the women remain in the same apartment with the
frustrated writer. Their unceasing chatter is a "more delicate
noise," but one which will last all day and, therefore, a "hopeless
noise." Thus the apparent relief implied in the word "delicate"
is canceled.

So far, all that happened took place in the real world. With
good-natured irony, the suffering hero describes the noises accompanying the morning activities of a middle-class family with
grown-up children and their effect on him. But suddenly the
helpless victim of the noisy family thinks of an old plan how
to fight back. All of this seems to lead to some "natural" con-
clusion of the sketch, but in the middle of a sentence Kafka
transposes the action into an unreal world in which a man can
crawl "snakelike" through a small crack in the barely opened
door and talk, frightfully metamorphosed, to his sisters, scaring
them terribly and yet asking them in the humblest way, that is,
by crawling on the floor, to be quiet. This transposition into a
metaphorical world says more than a realistic termination of this
sketch might have done.

Without having been told, the reader senses the complexity
of the situation. The passive narrator, so far requiring compassion
because he had suffered attack after attack on his nerves, now
threatens to attack, in turn. He intends to be more cruel than
those who hurt him. While they acted out of ignorance or forced
by necessity, he will act to revenge himself by suddenly frightening them and, at the same time, shame them with his humble
request humbly delivered.

The latent father-son conflict now takes on a new meaning.
Although the son does not strike back at the father, but only
at the father's party, the peculiar nature of this struggle between
the crawling snake and the trampling bull becomes clear; even
though the timid son only thinks of an old plan for a counter-
attack, it remains doubtful whether he will ever act.

As the "Letter to his Father" shows, this aspect of the little
sketch also reflects Kafka's life. In the "Letter," which was written

eight years later, he let his father defend himself: "I admit that we fight with each other, but there are two kinds of fighting. There is chivalrous fighting, in which the forces of independent opponents are measured against each other. . . . And there is the fighting of vermin."[16]

"Grosser Lärm," more than anything Kafka had previously written for publication, is the beginning of what he called his "inner biography." In a letter written a year later, he refers to the little prose piece as the "description of the acoustic conditions of our apartment, which has just appeared in a Prague periodical as a mild public chastisement of my family."[17]

"Grosser Lärm" is much more, however; it is the first mani-festation of Kafka's fully developed style. From now on, he will use fantastically changed reality in varied combinations with ordinary reality, as his next finished work, "Das Urteil," illustrates.

CHAPTER 4

The Sons

I Condemned to Death

ALTHOUGH Kafka never again wrote anything as directly autobiographical as "Grosser Lärm," his own problematic existence remained the main inspiration for his novels and stories. He himself recognized the autobiographical character of his work, calling it "the representation of my dreamlike inner life" in one of the many passages reflecting this aspect of his writing.

His first complete narrative after the breakthrough to his own style was "Das Urteil" ("The Judgment"), which he, usually so critical of his own work, praised unreservedly, analyzed in his diary, and commented upon in his letters to his fiancée. He went so far as to describe in his diary the circumstances under which the strange tale originated:

This story, *The Judgment*, I wrote at one sitting during the night of the 22nd–23rd, from ten o'clock at night to six o'clock in the morning. . . . The fearful strain and joy, how the story developed before me, as if I were advancing over water. . . . How everything can be said, how for everything, for the strangest fancies, there waits a great fire in which they perish and rise up again. . . . As the maid walked through the anteroom for the first time I wrote the last sentence. Turning out the light and the light of day. The slight pains around my heart. The weariness that disappeared in the middle of the night. The trembling entrance into my sisters' room. Reading aloud. . . . The conviction verified that with my novel-writing I am in the shameful lowlands of writing. Only *in this way* can writing be done, only with such coherence, with such a complete opening out of the body and the soul. . . . Many emotions carried along in the writing, joy, for example, that I shall have something beautiful for Max's *Arkadia*, thoughts about Freud, of course; . . . of course, also of my "The Urban World."[1]

This fragmentary prose piece, "Die städtische Welt" ("The Urban World"), and, to a lesser degree, "Grosser Lärm," are, as sketches, anticipatory of "Das Urteil." In the fragment, as in "Das Urteil," only three characters appear: Oscar, condemned as a dissolute son, his father, and Oscar's friend. The mother is still alive, but does not appear, belonging, like the mother in "Das Urteil" and "Die Verwandlung" ("Metamorphosis"), and like Kafka's own mother, entirely to the power sphere of the father.

The father-son conflict in "Die städtische Welt" and "Das Urteil" is decisively different from that depicted in the many literary works concerned with the same motif. Neither father nor son reflect aspects of the time in which Kafka lived, the last years before the First World War. The son in "Das Urteil," Georg Bendemann, is, moreover, neither an artist nor a quester nor an intellectual, as the rebelling sons in Western literature usually are. He is a businessman with good prospects, satisfied with his work, but made insecure by inner problems.

"Das Urteil" begins on a Sunday morning in spring with Georg writing a letter to a friend in Russia, informing him of his engagement; it ends on the same Sunday morning with his self-execution at the command of his father, who dies immediately before him.

The story's quick movement toward catastrophe and its growing tension and the concentration of the plot, are not the only dramatic elements of Kafka's style.[2] Kafka suppresses the authorial voice as much as possible and rather has gestures and dialogue indicate the feelings of his characters. The "absentminded slowness" with which Bendemann puts the letter into the envelope, the unseeing stare out of the window, the feeble smile at the acquaintance waving to him from the street—all these are dramatic gestures indicative of his inner disturbance. He is musing about the letter he just wrote to a childhood friend in Russia, an unsuccessful man whose business is on the decline. In *style indirect libre*[3] Georg's indecision is revealed: "What could one write to such a man who had obviously run off the rails, a man one could be sorry for but could not help. Should one advise him to come home? ..."[4] There follows a list of actions which Georg could take to save his friend; but he realizes their futility.

Georg's reflections about the unfortunate man's chances of

success show the same insincerity discernible in his past letters
to his friend, who noticed it and, when informed about Mrs.
Bendemann's death, answered with a very unemotional letter
of condolence. The narrator comments ironically: "The grief
caused by such an event . . . could not be realized in a distant
country."[5] Although expressed indirectly, this is the first rejection
Georg suffers in the story.

Much more severe is the second rejection, which comes from
his fiancée Frieda. When he appears before her as the smiling
young conqueror and tells her about the difficulty of informing
his friend of their engagement, his pity for the man's solitary
return to Russia after the wedding makes him suddenly ask:
"Alone—do you know what that means?"[6] She completely ignores
the implication, which should alert her, since smiling conquerors
do not know loneliness.

Frieda is portrayed as a sensitive girl; yet she is not interested
in what ails him, and her suggestion that he should not have
become engaged at all if he has that kind of friends is still
another indication of her weak or fading love. To pacify her,
Georg had written the letter with the important news of his
engagement to "a girl from a well-to-do family." According to
this cliché, he might be adjudged a philistine were it not for
signs of the awakening sensitivity which makes him lonely and
insecure among his own class. This insecurity is displayed when
he enters his father's bedroom to tell him about the letter. Now
the conquering hero appears belatedly as the devoted son, solicitous about his father's health and comfort, although he had not
been in the bedroom for several months.

As described by the narrator, the relations between the old
widower and the young bachelor have been peaceful enough
in their boring normality. The two men live in the same house
and work together in the same office, where the son is gradually
taking over the greater part of the responsibilities for the firm.
They have lunch together in a restaurant, and after supper, when
the son is at home, they read the newspaper in the living room.

This normality disappears as different metamorphoses of the
father take place: " 'Ah, Georg,' said the father, rising at once
to meet him. His heavy dressing gown sprung open as he walked
and the skirts of it fluttered around him—'My father is still a

giant,' said Georg to himself."[7] Georg uses the metaphorical term
"giant" to describe the outer appearance of his father, but then
he notices how sick and feeble the latter is. He begins to undress
him, all the time trying to persuade him that the Russian friend
really exists, while old Bendemann, in a feigned but insistent
argument, denies it.

As the old man is ready for bed, a new implied metaphor
evokes a bewildering scene: "He carried his father to bed in
his arms. It gave him a dreadful feeling to notice that while
he took the few steps towards the bed the old man on his breast
was playing with his watch chain. He could not lay him down
on the bed for a moment, so firmly did he hang on to the
watch chain."[8]

The words metaphorically implied in this passage might be
"baby" or "infantile idiot." The opposites "giant"—"baby" are
the two aspects of Kafka's own father, outwardly a giant, but
sometimes, in his moods and attitudes, a stubborn infant in the
eyes of his writer-son. But this metaphor is further extended.
The metaphorical child (or idiot) is acted upon and acts as if
it were real within the reality of the story; it is being carried
to bed, it holds on to the watchchain, as babies do. Here appears,
fully developed, the "Kafkaesque" aspect of Kafka's style: metaphors developed according to their implications, and unreal
situations and happenings fused with the real world of the story
out of which they develop.

In bed, the infant becomes old Bendemann again. As soon
as he has been tucked in by Georg, he asks if he is well "covered
up." The German participle *zugedeckt* ("covered up") means
both tucked-in and put *hors de combat*. Almost all critics miss
this meaning, substituting "to bury," which is wrong. At Georg's
reassuring answer, the father throws off his blanket, stands up-
right in bed, a bogeyman, and from on high pours out the envy
and hatred he feels for his son.

He now declares that he not only knows the friend in Russia,
of whom he says: "He would have been a son after my own
heart," but is allied with him against Georg. Then he ridicules
his son's engagement, matching his words with a pantomime
performed in his nightshirt, saying with a mincing voice: "'Because she lifted her skirts like this, the disgusting goose . . . you

made up to her, and in order to make free with her undisturbed
you have disgraced your mother's memory, betrayed your friend
and stuck your father into bed so he can't move. But he can
move, or can't he?' And he stood up quite unsupported and
kicked his legs out."[9]

The vicious demon dancing in bed now ridicules the son's claim
of being a good businessman: "And my son strutting through
the world, finishing off deals that I had prepared for him, . . .
stalking away from his father with the closed face of a respect-
able business man!"[10]

After this last attack, the "solicitous" son reacts strongly, but
only in his mind: "Now he'll lean forward, thought Georg. What
if he topples and smashes himself! These words went hissing
through his mind."[11]

Now the father, the giant, the baby, the evil demon of the
previous scenes, appears in his last, most frightful form. As
judge over life and death, he pronounces his verdict: "An innocent child, yes, that you were, truly, but still more truly have
you been a devilish human being!—And therefore take note: I
sentence you now to death by drowning!"[12] But the judge has
also condemned himself to death:

Georg felt himself urged from the room, the crash with which his
father fell on the bed behind him was still in his ears as he fled.
On the staircase, which he rushed down as if its steps were an
inclined plane, he ran into his charwoman on her way up to do
the morning cleaning of the room. . . . Out of the front door he
rushed, across the roadway, driven toward the water. Already he
was grasping at the railings as a starving man clutches food. He
swung himself over, like the distinguished gymnast he had once
been in his youth, to his parents' pride. With weakening grip he
was still holding on when he spied between the railings a motor-bus
coming which would easily cover the noise of his fall, called in a
low voice: "Dear parents, I have always loved you, all the same,"
and let himself drop.

At this moment an unending stream of traffic was just going
over the bridge.[13]

II *"Das Urteil"—A Metaphor*

Grotesque as the father may appear, he is not as far removed
from the reality of nineteenth-century fathers as modern readers

might think. There were many real characters who, in a hysterical rage, uttering curses like Old Testament patriarchs, would send a pregnant daughter or wayward son into exile. Even the death sentence pronounced by a father is not unheard of considering the time in which the story was written. Thus André Gide includes among the miscellany he picked up here and there for possible use in his novel *The Counterfeiters* the following item: "The pastor, upon learning that his son at twenty-six is no longer the chaste youth he thought him to be, exclaims: 'Would to heaven he had been killed in the war! Would to God he had never been born!' "[14]

Not for old Bendemann's violent wrath, but for the deeply disturbed father-son relation there exist parallels in Kafka's life at that time. In an answer to Felice's question about his position in the family Kafka stated in November, 1912, that he and his father hated each other with a vengeance. Yet he was too sensitive a man not to know about the injustice of this hatred. He also knew that what he felt for his father was *Hassliebe* ("love-hatred"). Later, in August, 1913, he appraised the situation more fairly: "You know that he is my enemy and I his, as is determined by our temperaments, but apart from this, my admiration for him as a man is perhaps as great as my fear of him. I can manage to avoid him; but ignore him, never."[15] He does not mention here that he felt sorry for his father because of old Kafka's unstable health. In spite of his robust appearance, the big man suffered from ailments which caused him and his family much worry. But even without this additional point, the above letter describes the apparent live model of the relation between fictional father and son.

Kafka also endowed his hero with his deep feelings of guilt, which were not as metaphysical as is often assumed, and not as far removed from actual guilt either. In an earlier letter he confessed: "The family's harmony is really upset only by me, and more so as the years go by; very often I don't know what to do, and feel a great sense of guilt towards my parents and everyone else."[16] He considered his guilt serious enough to condemn himself to death in his mind: "On more than one occasion in the past, I have stood by the window at night playing with the catch, feeling it almost my duty to open the window and throw myself out."[17]

Among Kafka's frequent suicidal phantasies about throwing himself out of windows there is one about dropping himself into the wintry Moldau, but about this suicide he speaks in a jocular tone. In January or February, 1908, he complained in a letter to a young girl student, with whom he carried on a half-amorous correspondence, about his work in the Italian insurance company and adds: "Last week I really was a suitable inhabitant of the street in which I am living and which I call 'Running Start Street for Suicides,' for this broad street leads to a river, where a bridge is being built . . . but I say all that only in jest."[18] The bridge was finished in 1912 when Kafka had young Bendemann jump from it.

Many readers admit that this story has a certain fascination for them but complain that it seems to be too exaggerated and unreal. How many fathers would condemn their sons to death? How many sons would commit suicide at their father's command? Probably very few, but that is not what Kafka conveys in this story. As the first to comment on it, he points out, in his diaries, the close connection between the story and his life by explaining the names Georg Bendemann and Frieda Brandenfeld as cryptograms of his own and Felice Bauer's name.[19] Since he had dedicated "Das Urteil" to his future fiancée, Felice Bauer, he occasionally discusses the story in his letters to her, which were unpublished until 1967 (and in English translation until 1970) and hence unknown to many Kafka critics. A little over two months after the productive September night he writes: "But you don't even know your little story 'The Judgment' yet. It is somewhat wild and meaningless and if it didn't express some inner truth (which can never be universally established, but has to be accepted or denied every time by each reader or listener in turn), it would be nothing."[20] It would be nothing but a grotesque tale if the story were taken literally. What the characters say and do is generally implausible, lacks "outer truth," while expressing metaphorically "inner truth." Old Bendemann's playing with the watchchain, his antics in the bed, and then again the biblical ring of the subjunctive introducing the judgment ('Und darum wisse" ["And therefore know thou"]), the judgment itself, and the son's self-execution—all these express metaphorically an "inner reality," the "feel" of the relation between father and son, and also between Franz and Herrmann Kafka. Only in such a metaphorical sense are Kafka's stories autobiographical: the businessman, schoolboy, traveling salesman, bank clerk, land surveyor, these show people, and reasoning animals are not modeled after Kafka the writer or official but are characters whose struggles, anxieties, and defeats are metaphors for his inner experiences, complex feelings requiring of the reader empathetic understanding.

Despite its sober prose, Kafka's work frequently borders on poetry due to its strictly metaphoric character. He himself felt this with regard to "Das Urteil" when he wrote to his publisher: "Die Erzählung ist mehr gedichtmässig als episch" ("the story has more of a lyric than epic character").[21] The truly lyric creation can never be translated into conceptual language, and in this sense Kafka wrote Felice about the little tale he had dedicated to her: "The 'Judgment' cannot be explained. Perhaps one day I'll show you some entries in my diary about it. The story is full of abstractions, though they are never admitted. The friend is hardly a real person, perhaps he is more whatever the father and Georg have in common. The story may be a journey around father and son, and the friend's changing shape may be a change in perspective in the relationship between father and son. But I am not quite sure of this, either."[22]

The term "abstractions not revealed as such" refers to the metaphors not set off from the *concrete*, that is, realistic, part of the story. Kafka was the opposite of an abstract thinker; he had no philosophical talent. As he himself admitted, he "thought in images," and the meaning of the word "abstract," as used here, is the more popular one: unreal, existing in thought only. When he says that "the friend is scarcely a real person" he does not mean that he does not exist, but that he is not developed as a character, as the two Bendemanns are, and that his function is simply to show the complex relation between father and son, the real content of the story. "Das Urteil" reveals its inner truth through its unreal scenes. It is "wild and meaningless" only if the father, as senior director of the firm, patron of a restaurant, reader of the evening paper, is visualized on the same level of

reality as when he becomes a baby, reads the defunct newspaper,
and condemns his son to death. Only the "wild" abstractions,
that is, metaphors and phantastic scenes, reveal the inner truths:
what the characters really feel, how the relations of father and
son really are. The son, confronted with his father, is no longer
the young successful businessman, conqueror of "a girl from a
well-to-do family"; he is alone and perturbed, without the power
to love either his father, a friend, or his fiancée, but with the
power to hate his father so fiercely that he wishes him killed
by a fall against the edge of the bed. "Now he'll lean forward,
thought Georg, what if he topples and smashes himself!"[23] This
devilish wish is fulfilled. Georg carries away in his ears the
crash with which his father, collapsing, strikes the bed. The
orgy of mutual hatred ends with this crash. Then, during the few
seconds in which Georg clears the railing and hangs above the
water, we envision him at a gymnastic festival distinguishing
himself, to the delight of his parents, at a time when his world
was untainted by hatreds and contempts. Young Bendemann's
melancholy reminiscence ends with his last words: "Dear parents,
I always did love you." The whole story in its "inner truth"
was a confession that Kafka, the son, felt urged to make in these
years when his relations with both his father and mother were
particularly bad. The desire to achieve reconciliation with his
father stayed with him throughout life. In 1917 he formulated
that wish almost like an epilogue to "Das Urteil": "I would put
myself in death's hands, though. Remnant of a faith. Return to
the father. Great day of reconciliation."[24]

"The inner truth," a basic concept in Kafka's literary criticism,
does not mean in his own work a religious or philosophical
insight but rather the revelation of his own inner experience:
in "Das Urteil," of the disturbed relation to his father, the
Hassliebe ("love-hatred") each felt for the other. It was this
inner truth that struck Kafka both at a public reading of the
story and a private one at the home of his writer friend Oskar
Baum: "There were tears in my eyes. The indubitability [inner
truth] of the story was confirmed."[25] It might well be that the
passage "Dear parents, I always did love you" provoked these
tears. He had expressed the same feeling a year and a half earlier
in "Die städtische Welt," and three months later he expressed

it again at the end of "Die Verwandlung." Obviously that late confession of filial love meant much to him.

III *"Das Urteil"—An Allegory*

If after having read Kafka's remarks about any of his works, one consults older commentaries about them, one has the feeling that they were written about another author, and not by literary critics but by scholastics. The earliest critics sometimes forgot that Kafka wrote in German, that he was not a Czech national, and that he was a Jew and not a Christian. Sometimes they did not read the text carefully in their eagerness to philosophize about it.

These were the critics of the forties and of the early fifties. The friend in Russia, according to one early critic,[26] is the inner self of Kafka, the writer. The fact that the gas fixtures are dangling from the ceiling in his plundered shop means that Kafka wrote by gaslight (he did not). The friend with his yellow complexion, indicating a latent disease, looks ready "to be tossed out," as the father says. This is allegorically explained: Kafka accumulated his manuscripts until they were yellow enough to be tossed away. In the same essay, dedicated to "Das Urteil," the critic asserts: "In *The Judgment*, as in *The Castle*, Kafka's father is the Father-God, at once terrible and desirable, ineludible and unattainable, incomprehensible and uncomprehending." The author forgot that this God is also mortal and dies in bed.

The next period in Kafka criticism was dominated by four German scholars[27] who published their voluminous books, from 400 to 500 pages in length, between 1958 and 1965 in Germany, two of them also publishing an English version in the United States. One of these critics represents best the desire of Kafka commentators to interpret away everything that is "merely psychological," realistic, typical of a certain time and place, and to discover, instead, universal and metaphysical meanings. He wards off the purely secular interpretation of the friend's relation to Georg and the father, saying of its author's explanation: "As a typical Kafka commentary, this diary entry is apt to complicate and obfuscate the basic relationships around which the story is constructed."[28] The opposite seems to be true, but if Kafka's own interpretations are accepted, the critic warns his colleagues, "We move from the universal meaning of the story back to its psychological motivations and reduce the stature of the friend from the metaphysical to the merely interesting and ephemeral."[29] Any secularization of a Kafka text is considered blasphemous in this "metaphysical" school. The same critic elevates Bendemann Senior from the lowly position of an "Oedipal tyrant" to that of a godlike figure, endowed with omniscience, omnipotence, and the authority of absolute jurisdiction. In addition, this critic understands *zudecken* to mean "to bury" and resurrects his godlike father in the character of "a primitive war god."[30] This elevation is bestowed upon Bendemann because of a scar on his thigh from his war years.

In keeping with the two apotheoses is a mystical time change: "From a Sunday, when in Kafka's Europe the streets were deserted, Georg has moved through the timelessness of his encounter with the father to a Monday, when life resumes its business, the charwoman climbs up the stairs to begin the work of a new week."[31] "Charwomen," to be sure, do not come into the house on Sunday; the original says "seine Bedienerin" ("his maidservant"). This maidservant does not come to "do the morning cleaning of the room,"[32] as the English translation says. She comes "to tidy up the rooms after the night." The critic has committed, like many of his colleagues, the mistake of relying on a translation, an unadvisable procedure, particularly in Kafka's case. Neither is the heavy traffic over the bridge Monday traffic; many excursionists hike or ride on this beautiful Sunday morning across the bridge to reach the Belvedere and the heights on the other bank "with their tender green." Time has not mystically changed in the presence of the war god Bendemann.

Georg, too, has his metaphysical aspects, according to this commentary: "... The judgment, leaving psychology behind, speaks of the close interconnection, in every human being, of good and evil. . . . of the devil entering the world of divine creation."[33] This "close interconnection of good and evil" reduces Georg's uniqueness to a psychological commonplace, but the father singles him out as a "devilish human being." The devil could only have entered divine creation if the contradictory characteristic of Georg, innocent-devilish, had been successive; but the two qualities coexist. And even then it would have been a psychological process, and not a cosmic event, if the child Georg had grown up to be a sinister character.

Kafka considered the antinomy innocent/guilty as typical of himself. In December, 1912, he wrote: "Innocent, and certainly guilty as well, I am locked up, not in a cell, but in this town."[34] Again this antinomy appears in his diary entry of July, 1914. Describing his meeting with Felice's parents in the hotel aimed at persuading them that breaking off his engagement with Felice would be the best solution for them both, the master of the word, the practiced lawyer, easily defeated the two simple people and was ashamed: "They agreed that I was right, there was nothing, or not much, that could be said against me. Devilish in all innocence."[35]

Not willing to grant the hero a merely human character, the critic finds fault with Georg's last words "Dear parents, I always did love you" as flawing the story: "He [Georg] remains deaf to the metaphysical depth of the judgment and succumbs simply to old Bendemann's suddenly resuscitated will."[36] But Georg is not succumbing to his father's hypnotic powers, but rather to his feelings of guilt which had been saddening him long before that fateful Sunday morning when his father intensifies these feelings until they become unbearable.

After the characters have been elevated, their outer world is raised to mystical heights: "Perhaps one could see in the last sentence [of the story] a symbolic resumption of the city's commerce which had been temporarily halted by Georg's activities. Perhaps Kafka even meant this city to represent the world, a generalization that offered itself easily to him."[37]

After such godlike fathers, war gods, and cities which mean the world, any statement made by Kafka himself about his stories sounds too humble to be true. Four and a half months after he had written "The Judgment," he read it at the home of his friend Weltsch. Father Weltsch, as Kafka reports, had left for a moment after the reading, and when he came back he said: " 'I see this father before me,' all the time looking directly at the empty chair in which he had been sitting while I was reading. My sister said: 'It is our apartment.' I was astonished how mistaken she was in the setting and said, 'In that case, then, father would have to be living in the toilet.' "[38]

Disappointed, the above-quoted critic comments: "If we are correct in assuming that in *The Judgment* Kafka had intended to create a new myth of the father . . . then he defeated his own purpose by commentaries and interpretations of this kind. . . . Whether he sincerely attempted to solve the problems he had posed while writing *The Judgment* or whether he poked fun at the listeners who identified themselves all too easily with the products of his imagination, we are unable to decide today."[39]

It is difficult to see any "fun-poking" in the quoted remarks. The old Weltsch was not addressed by Kafka, and the correction of his sister's wrong interpretation does not sound amused, but rather a little impatient. Moreover, Kafka was not the "fun-poking" type.

The most complex allegorist among the four German critics mentioned does not allow any of Kafka's works to be set in a city inhabited by mortals, even if this city incorporated the whole world. Kafka deals, as he expresses it, with "the infinite universe of human religious concepts in the West,"[40] with which this critic interprets everything and anybody in his author's works. Georg Bendemann is a claimant to a messianic mission, the mother the dead Jewish faith, the father, collapsing in bed, is the God-image of the Old Testament, the dark room, closed on all sides "alludes to the holy of holies in the Jewish temple,"[41] and so forth.

Psychoanalytical criticism is another method used by critics to give Kafka's works universal validity. One recent practitioner of this school asserted in 1968: "What the story is about is Georg's struggle against his 'neurotic' submission to his father's 'comic' pretensions to absolute authority; it is a 'psychoanalytic' story through and through."[42] But the father's claim to have established the firm is not comic, Georg's death wish for the father is no neurotic submission, and the love expressed in Georg's last words makes such an Oedipal interpretation appear too simple. Those tender last words are interpreted by the psychoanalytical critic as a sign that "the helpless Georg" is succumbing to his father's wish. He thus interprets them negatively, just like the critic who considered them detrimental to the universal meaning of the story. Disagreements as to whether certain characters and their actions are to be considered good or bad are typical of Kafka criticism and will be discussed again.

The same psychoanalyzing critic also relies on allegory and strained symbolism: "The darkness [in the father's room] is the interior darkness of his own [Georg's] self."[43] The covers which the father flings off [he only flings off one cover] "are all those trappings of civilization which conceal the primitive battle to the death between fathers and sons. Suddenly we are pitched out of history back into natural history...."[44] The father is now called by the critic "this tribal *Urvater*, this hunting forefather,"[45] although old Bendemann boasts of customers he acquired, not of mammoths he hunted. The antinomy: innocent child–devilish man is, again, no longer considered as being characteristic for Georg, but for all males: "... In reaching for a wife he [Georg] oversteps the 'law' which gives all wives to the father, and he becomes a 'devil.' Child or devil is the alternative his father confronts him with."[46] And thus another Kafka story has lost all specific meaning, to become a Freudian allegory of mating Western men.

IV *Metamorphosed*

While the young businessman Georg Bendemann is condemned to death in Kafka's metaphorical world, the young commercial traveler Gregor Samsa in "Die Verwandlung" ("The Metamorphosis") must live out the last months of his life in the same world changed as a giant bug, which resembles a cockroach.

Compared with "Die Verwandlung," the little prose piece "Grosser Lärm" appears like a first sketch for the larger story. The characterization of father and son is the same: the father is the mighty master of the family, and the son, living helplessly in their midst, frightens them in his monstrous shape. "Grosser Lärm" appeared in October, 1912, in a Prague magazine; and on November 11 Kafka sent a copy to Felice. The little prose piece was fresh in his mind when, six days later, waiting in bed for a letter from her, the idea for "Die Verwandlung" came to him in his "wretchedness." As in "Das Urteil," which preceded it, the inspiration for "Die Verwandlung" was his unhappy family life, which was only eased somewhat by his sister Ottla, who also defied the father and tried to help her unfortunate brother.

"Die Verwandlung" opens with the sentence: "As Gregor

Samsa awoke one morning from uneasy dreams he found himself
transformed in his bed into a gigantic insect."[47] The dependent
clause tells us of the real world, and—such is Kafka's subtle
style—something important about the hero's previous life. The
main clause shifts immediately to Gregor's metaphorical state.
During the last night, in which he had fallen asleep in bed
as a man, Gregor had "uneasy dreams," the result of an inner
unrest; and his thoughts upon awakening reveal what caused
them. He complains about the physical discomfort of the commercial traveler, but also about something much more important,
about the dehumanizing effect of his job due to the always
changing human contacts, which never lead to close personal
relations. Worst of all, he feels humiliated by the head of the
firm, who has the disgusting habit of sitting on a high desk, so
he can talk down to his employees. Although by ordinary literary
and human standards a miserable creature, this man shares with
many another authoritative character the divine honors bestowed
upon him by an allegorizer: "The description of Gregor's boss
has breadth enough to apply not just to a petty office tyrant,
but even to an [sic] Old Testament God. Indeed, the reference
to the high desk echoes the Old Testament metaphor of the
God 'most high' who yet can 'hear' us."[48] This "petty office tyrant"
would fulminate against Gregor should he be late for work.
Since, as Gregor firmly believes, his parents owe his employer
money he has to stay with the despised job for five or six
more years.

Such reflections have occupied Gregor's mind for some while
before the catastrophe and have made him lose faith in himself
and in the rightness of his life, as had also happened to Georg
Bendemann. In the author's fictitious world, Gregor has become
what he had metaphorically been for a long time: an insect.

As if to ward off subsequent critical misinterpretation of the
events described in this story as nightmares of a neurotic, the
narrator explains in the second sentence: "It was no dream:
his room, a regular bedroom, only rather too small, lay quiet
between the four familiar walls."[49] Gregor had his breakthrough
to self-recognition, and the implied metaphor—something like "I
am really a spineless bug"—is at once fused with the realistically
described life he leads between the four walls of his room.

On one of these hangs Gregor's "pinup," a testimony to his sense of inferiority. It is a cutout from some illustrated magazine, representing a lady of wealth, high above his rank, wearing a fur stole and "holding out to the spectator a huge fur muff, in which the whole of her forearm had vanished."[50] Fur stoles, it should be noted, were considered by some in prewar Europe to be ostentatious status symbols, and Kafka detested them. He once informed Grete Bloch: "One has some convictions that are so deep-seated and true that one doesn't have to worry about a detailed justification. . . . I don't have many convictions of this kind," and then he mentions two of them: "the abomination of contemporary medicine, and . . . the ugliness of the fur stole."[51]

Gregor's fur-clad idol is enclosed in a gilded frame which the young commercial traveler has cut out with a fretsaw, fretwork, a hobby usually associated with boys rather than grown-up men, being the only luxury he allows himself. Otherwise his arid life consists of sitting at home every evening, reading the paper, or studying timetables, so that he may beat the competition by taking earlier trains.

His metamorphosis, of course, makes him miss all the trains on this fateful morning, and the manager, informed by the firm's porter, who spies on the salesmen, arrives at the home of the Samsas. In vain Mrs. Samsa attempts to pacify him. Suspecting that Gregor might be a malingerer, or, still worse, that he was about to make off with some company funds, he displays his art of humiliating his inferiors before the embarrassed family of his employee.

Gregor, still struggling to get out of bed and open the door, is incapable of making himself understood with his beetle mouth, but has kept his human understanding and feeling. At last he succeeds in dropping down on the floor. Lying there for a while helplessly on his back, he has a humorous thought:

Gregor tried to suppose to himself that something like what had happened to him today might someday happen to the chief clerk; one really could not deny that it was possible. But as if in brusque reply to his supposition the chief clerk took a couple of firm steps in the next-door room and made his patent leather boots creak.[52]

The "crude answer" is clear. A man who walks on patent-leather shoes during a work day walks on status symbols and is in no danger of ever losing confidence in himself.

The assertion that "one really had to admit that possibility" that the manager would some day awaken as a bug is typical of Kafka's wry humor; at the same time, it hints at the possibility that a human being may awaken to the insight that he is a "bug," a person without character and, consequently, without human dignity. The manager is a malicious, conceited man who, without any knowledge of himself, derives the firmness of his steps solely from the awareness of his patent-leather shoes and all they stand for in his world of spurious values. But Kafka knew that there were people who walked through life with firm steps, and justifiably so. Less than a year after he wrote "Die Verwandlung," the metaphor of such "authentic" firm steps appears in his diary, where, as in his letters, he used metaphors occurring in his literary works. The entry reads: "The unimaginable sadness in the morning. In the evening read Jacobsohn's *Der Fall Jacobsohn.* [Siegfried Jacobsohn was a publicist of about Kafka's age.] This strength to live, to make decisions, joyfully to set one's foot in the right place. He sits in himself the way a practiced rower sits in his boat and would sit in any boat...."[53] On the same day he reread "Die Verwandlung."

Kafka admired men like the author Jacobsohn of the firm steps who is, of course, in firmness and decision the opposite of Gregor and his author. There was, however, a time when Gregor took firm steps like the manager, and though he never wore patent-leather shoes and fine clothes, he wore then something incomparably nobler, a lieutenant's uniform. The beetleman's first excursion out of his room ends in the living room, and there on the wall just opposite him "hung a photograph of himself in military service, as a lieutenant, hand on sword, a carefree smile on his face, inviting one to respect his uniform and military bearing."[54]

After the "fur uniform" of the proud lady, and lieutenant Gregor Samsa's uniform, a third one appears in this story. As long as Gregor was working, the father had enjoyed a premature dotage, but since Gregor's misfortune he has shaken off his senility and has become the porter of a bank, clad in a uniform with golden buttons, which soon looks soiled since he never takes it off before bedtime. This "servant-uniform" strengthens the old man to such a degree that he would have killed the metamorphosed son in a fit of rage by trampling upon him or bombarding him with apples if the mother had not intervened.

"Die Verwandlung" offers the worst example of the disagreement among Kafka's critics as to the moral qualities of his characters. Strangely enough, nobody mentions the patent fact that the people surrounding the metamorphosed Gregor are the real vermin while he begins to rise even before his misfortune. His "uneasy dreams" are the beginning of his development from a timid nothing of a man believing in spurious values to a true human being. There is a gathering of vermin in Gregor's firm: the boss's way of humiliating the employees has been mentioned. The porter, the lowliest creature in the firm, watches at the railroad station, so that he can report to him whether the commercial travelers took the earliest possible train or not. Samsa thinks about him as of an insect: "He was a creature of the chief's, spineless and stupid."[55] The manager well represents the firm, driving Gregor and his family to despair with his false concern and vicious innuendoes. The Italian insurance company had provided Kafka with models for that kind of bug.

The worst insect among the vermin in the story is, however, the parasitical father. Although he knew how his son loathed his employment with the firm to whose principal old Samsa owed money, he never told him that he had saved enough from his bankruptcy and from Gregor's earnings, so that Gregor might have ended his debtor's slave work years earlier than would have been possible under the present conditions.

Among the "real" vermin, Gregor's sister is the only exception, at least during the first weeks after his metamorphosis, when she lovingly experiments with food until she knows what her unfortunate brother likes to eat; but then she begins to neglect him more and more. At the same time, Gregor loses his appetite and hardly touches his food any longer. To make his suffering worse, a maid has been hired, an uncouth, rawboned big female who embitters him by addressing him as "old crap beetle."[56] Finally the parents have taken three lodgers into the house, Chaplinesque characters whom he watches while they are eating.

" 'I'm hungry enough,' said Gregor sadly to himself, 'but not
for that kind of food. How these lodgers are stuffing themselves,
and here am I dying of starvation!' "[57]

This is no longer the Gregor who admired status symbols,
who clung to the cheap picture in his room, fearing it might be
removed. The vulgarity of his former life has disappeared, and
the food the three roomers are eating with such audible gusto
is no longer just food but a symbol of all that pleases and
nourishes them as human beings. Gregor can no longer be
satisfied with the "grub" of their lives and the lives of those
like them, as he had been before. The unbridgeable gap between
him and people like these becomes clear when his sister plays
the violin before them. Since the dullards cannot understand
the serious music she has chosen, they boorishly show their
contempt for this kind of entertainment, although the young girl
reveals all her devotion to music in the way she plays.

This small example of the barbarian's contempt for the language of the arts has provoked, through the ages, many protests
like the following one by Goethe, which will help to explain
what Gregor is hungering for: "The people do not appreciate
us [the artists] if we increase their inner need [Kafka calls it
hunger], give them a great ideal for their own selves, if we want
to make them feel how glorious a true, noble existence is."[58]

Gregor's inner needs are increased by her playing. His humiliation is approaching its end, his suffering has raised him to a
truly human level, and, for the first time since his metamorphosis,
he has good reason to doubt the justice of his frightful degrada-
tion. The question in which he expresses his doubt is essential
to the understanding of the story: "War er ein Tier, da ihn Musik
so ergriff?"[59] ("Could he really be an animal since music touched
him so?") The use of the conjunction *da* with adversative force
is very rare, and most German, and almost all English, critics
understood it in its usual causal function, many of them having
to rely on the two English translations in which *da* is also rendered as a causal particle. Nevertheless the commentators succeeded to wrest a meaning from the sibylline rhetorical question:
"Was he an animal, that music had such an effect upon him?"[60]

One of the four German scholars previously referred to calls
Gregor's question fittingly "the decisive sentence," but, tricked

by the *da* explains: "As an animal he is at the same time more than an animal."[61] Another German commentator, sensitive to the adversative meaning of *da*, wants nevertheless to save the causal meaning, explaining: "Gregor, about whom we learned earlier that he did not have so intimate a relation to music as his sister, now obtains it on the primitive-emotional basis of his animal organization and in so doing becomes more clearly conscious of being an animal as well."[62] That would make of Gregor, because of his all-encompassing inner life, a superman as well as a superbeetle. One lone commentator gives the correct translation, but then rules out the doubt in Gregor's question and asserts, correcting him: "On the contrary, it is just when he is an animal that music moves him: The totem is the deeper and better self."[63] After these strange metamorphoses of metamorphosed Gregor, the resigned statement of one critic who interprets *da* in the common, in this case the wrong, way may conclude this strange list: "In Kafka's unfathomable sentence: 'Was he an animal that music could move him so?' paradox echoes jarringly without end."[64] Strangely enough, this paradox, created by interpreters, does not exist in the French, Spanish, and Italian standard translations, where the decisive sentence is rendered correctly.

Gregor, listening, deeply moved, to his sister's violin playing, is now an animal only in his outer form; his inner being reveals a sensitive man, something he was not before, when, as a lieutenant, "he could demand respect for his bearing and uniform," and when later, as a commercial traveler, he stolidly accepted his soul-deadening job. He has reached the highest point in his life which, in its previous form, together with many other human qualities, lacked also interest in music. The violin playing of his sister gives him hope: "He felt as if the way were opening before him to the unknown nourishment he craved."[65]

No longer is the violin-playing sister the middle-class girl discussing with her mother the price of the nextdoor grocer's eggs and the mores of his daughter. While playing the violin, she has left the banality and ugliness of her own and her family's life; she is transfigured. Gregor feels how she is lifted out of this netherworld to which his firm, his parents, the three roomers, and the maid belong, and to which he, too, belonged until he awoke one morning from "uneasy dreams" as a beetle

feeding on rotten food. Beginning with this moment of greatest
humiliation, he began to rise until the "grub" with which those
around him sustained their lives no longer sustained his own,
since "his inner needs were increased," as Goethe said.

Having reached this elevated point, his life ends. Dying he
thinks "with love and compassion" of his family, just as Georg
Bendemann thought of his parents. The maid announces to the
older Samsas that the terrible nuisance has "croaked." They all
go to Gregor's room, and Grete, as the speaker of this strange
chorus surrounding the dead "hero," laments: "Just see how thin
he was. It's such a long time since he's eaten anything. The food
came out [was taken out] again just as it went in."[66] The parents
are too indifferent or too relieved to protect their son from a
last ignominy. His body has been left to the maid, who sweeps
"the stuff in the next room" away and drops it into the dust bin.

Just as for "Das Urteil," Kafka has provided a Fortinbras end
for "Die Verwandlung." Such an end, following the death of
the complex, suffering hero is an affirmation of simple life in
its brutality, but also in its beauty, which continues unabated
by all the tragedies among its "problem children." In "Das Urteil,"
a mighty stream of traffic across the bridge represents life, drowning out the plop with which unhappy Mr. Bendemann leaves it.
In "Die Verwandlung," the parents try to recuperate after Gregor's
death from the strains and horrors of the last weeks. Leaving
the town by streetcar, they realize that Grete, in spite of the
misfortune that had affected them all, has grown up to be a
beautiful, nubile girl: "And it was like a confirmation of their
new dreams and excellent intentions that at the end of their
journey their daughter sprang to her feet first and stretched her
young body."[67]

V   Metamorphosed Again

Whereas Grete has words of compassion for the dead hero,
most commentators who denigrate him dead and alive do not.
Obviously misled by the ambiguous translation "The food came
out again just as it went in" and without paying attention to
Grete's compassion, the best-known Kafka critic of the early
sixties writing in English misquotes: "The food came out of
him again just as it went in" and then reflects: "Grete likens

him here to a pipe, a lifeless object. He has not really lived; existence, physical and metaphysical, has moved through him and left no trace. The metamorphosis has failed to change him."[68] Others call Gregor a parasite "that saps the father's and the family's life,"[69] although as long as he could work he was the opposite. Gregor's rather obvious rise to a level high above his previous state is interpreted by some as a regression to beastliness. His uninteresting pinup lady with the fur accessories is, according to psychoanalyzing critics,[70] dressed in sex symbols and an object of the evil beetle's lust, just as his imagined attempts to show his sister the tenderness he feels for her are considered an incestuous reverie.

We will have further occasion to note that Kafka critics cannot agree on the evaluation of his characters. It seems the misunderstood "decisive sentence" has caused many to overlook Gregor's continuous rise toward the level of a truly "human" being even though his monstrous shape remains the same. That rise began before the metamorphosis took place, his uneasy dreams were caused by his inner unhappiness, which preceded his misfortune and gradually led him to crave the true food for his inner man. It is hard to see how the villains of the piece, the firm's porter, its president, its manager, and, most of all, the egotistic father, could have been missed as the true vermin in the story; one critic even praises the vicious manager, for commenting on Gregor's attempt to speak: "That was an animal's voice." The statement is, in that critic's opinion, a word of profoundest wisdom: "The junior manager, who is in some respects the realist of the story, here utters in four words Kafka's whole criticism both of himself and of mankind."[71] In defense of Gregor's rise to human heights it should also be mentioned that Kafka's stories, closely interrelated, usually have a redeeming end. If their heroes die, they do so on a level of being or insight higher than the one on which they lived.

When discussing critics writing before 1967 one should keep in mind that they could not benefit from studying Kafka's letters to Felice, which appeared in that year. Directly and indirectly Kafka speaks repeatedly in these letters about his first publications, before they were written, while they were being written, and after they appeared in print. In his letter and his diaries,

Kafka, more than other writers, anticipates the as yet unwritten work in metaphors dealing with its subject matter, mood, and sometimes even the small but revealing details destined to be used, although the author did not know it yet.

Much of "Die Verwandlung" is anticipated in a letter to Felice, written on November 1, 1912, sixteen days before the story was begun. In answer to her question about his "way of life," Kafka warns her that he would have to say some "scabrous things" about himself. Beginning with the confession that his life consists basically of attempts to write, he uses a strong metaphor which, in the story, was to describe Gregor's burial: "But when I didn't write, I was at once flat on the floor, fit for the dustbin."[72] His general weakness, he continues, made it necessary for him to deprive himself severely to save his strength on all sides, so that he would keep enough strength for this main purpose—writing. "When I didn't do so, . . . but tried to reach beyond my strength, I was automatically forced back, wounded, humbled, forever weakened."[73] He does not mention his father here, but every one of these verbs fits the treatment Kafka received from his father and, in a literary sense, Gregor from old Samsa, who had "forced back, wounded, and forever weakened" his monstrous son.

The next paragraph of the letter is an example of "Kafkaesque" style, of the smooth shift from reality to a metaphorical plane, applied, in this case, to the metaphors of hunger and becoming thin: "Just as I am thin, and I am the thinnest person I know (and that's saying something, for I am no stranger to sanatoria), there is also otherwise nothing to me which, in relation to writing, one could call superfluous, superfluous in the sense of overflowing."[74] He speaks, first, of his physical thinness and then immediately shifts the concept "thinness" to a metaphorical plane, the word "otherwise" indicating the shift. On the metaphorical plane, his thinness now means that there is no "superfluous" talent or energy or any other positive quality left in him. The double sense of "thinness" forms a parallel to the real and metaphorical sense of food in "Die Verwandlung." First it meant the food Gregor could eat after he was changed, whereas later on it is the life food toward which the violin-playing sister has shown him the way.

And what does this story mean? Of course, like any true work of literary art, it means more than its abstract scheme, that is, the development of a human being from a subhuman level, which is acceptable to the people of his world, to a superior level in a form unacceptable to them and to him, and from which only death can free him. Its meaning is expressed in the words which the author, not the critic, has chosen. The commentator can only help the reader to a closer understanding of motives and images and can clear up philological difficulties. He may do the close reading the works of an author like Kafka require if intellectual obstacles threaten to hinder the understanding of mood and feeling which an older writer like Kafka offers.

The reader himself must feel the humor in the scene where the chief clerk fills the well of the staircase with his shout of fear, while the bug man, rushing toward him on his many thin legs, only wants to excuse his unavoidable tardiness before his superior. The skilled reader, and the one who wants moral edification, will enjoy, each in his own way, the paradox that the "normal" people around Gregor are the vermin while he increasingly becomes a true human being in spite of his monstrous shape. The senile and yet tyrannical father, the Chaplin-esque lodgers, the tough maid, the slimy manager as well as the "invisible" characters—the employer at his high desk, the vicious porter, spying at the railroad station—all delight the reader who does not mind enjoying realistically but masterfully presented characters. Gregor's dissatisfaction is indirectly, but for that reason very powerfully, expressed by Kafka. It is not a social or political accusation, but the realization that it is very difficult to find in life the "food" which lifts the inner man above the banality of existence. The temptation is great to blame our modern times for being particularly hostile to the inner man and his hunger, but such cultural criticism is not Kafka's intention, as he had said himself. Besides, laments about the increasing dehumanization of life, its degeneration due to the utilitarian spirit of the age, were heard as long ago as the later eighteenth and early nineteenth centuries. In Germany, such protests were particularly passionate. There was a writer to whom not music but the Greeks had shown the way to the longed-for, unknown food which this poor Tantalus could never

reach: Friedrich Hölderlin, the author of a novel with the significant title: *Hyperion, or The Solitary in Greece*, expressed
Samsa's yearning, although in a totally different tone, in his
poem *Der Archipelagus*:

... and much do these barbarians work
with powerful arms, restlessly, but again and again
Barren like the Furies are the endeavors of these wretches
Until awakened, the soul returns to men from their frightening dream
Youthfully joyful....[75]

VI *Exiled*

"Das Urteil" had been the work of one September night, and
"Die Verwandlung" was finished in three weeks; but the novel
Amerika on which Kafka worked during the same creative year,
1912, and then again in 1914, remained a fragment. By 1913 he
had considered giving it up as a failure, exempting, however,
the first chapter which, he said, came from "inner truth." It was
this part of the novel which was published within his lifetime
under the title *Der Heizer* (The Stoker) (1913). Three years
after his death, in 1927, Brod published all the chapters and
fragments of chapters under the title *Amerika*.

Kafka's interest in the United States was nothing extraordinary. In the beginning of the century, there prevailed among
the German-speaking people lively, if contradictory, opinions
about the gigantic country of Indians, cowboys, and industrial
barons. Widely read, especially by the young, were Cooper's
Indian novels, *The Last of the Mohicans* becoming a slogan in
the German language. But white America was also considered
a half-wild country, rough enough to attract adventurers, men
of action, prodigal sons, and social outcasts; in short, all those
who did not like Europe or were not liked by it.

The yearning for "freedom in all directions" seems to have
turned Kafka's interest to America when he was still a student
at the *Gymnasium*. A lost novel at which he worked in those
early years dealt with two brothers, one of whom had gone to
America, while the other, significantly enough, was in Europe
in a prison. Particularly the Red Indian was to him a symbol
of freedom. In his first published book, *Betrachtung*, one of the

children whoops an Indian war cry, a common occurrence in those days. One of the sketches in the little book entitled *Wish to Become an Indian* shows Kafka daydreaming during his riding lessons, wishing the appurtenances of the modern European rider would disappear and he would gallop over the land unencumbered like an Indian. Most interesting is another sketch entitled "The Rejection," the first paragraph of which reveals much of Kafka's romantic notion of the States:

When I meet a pretty girl and beg her: "Be so good as to come with me," and she walks past without a word, this is what she means to say: "You are no Duke with a famous name, no broad American with a Red Indian figure, level, brooding eyes and a skin tempered by the air of the prairies and the rivers that flow through them, you have never journeyed to the Great Lakes and voyaged on them wherever they may be, I don't know where. So why, pray, should a pretty girl like myself go with you?"[76]

Today the calm eyes and unwrinkled face of the white American are a literary cliché, but the interpretation may also be negative. The same Kafka wrote in 1916, after not having touched his novel for almost two years, a few additional sentences for the last complete chapter. When two young Americans on a train laugh at the enthusiasm of his young hero Karl, he observes: "What kind of fellows were they and what did they know? Smooth American faces with only two or three wrinkles...."[77]

In 1911 and 1912, Kafka's knowledge of America was considerably enhanced by articles in the influential literary magazine *Die neue Rundschau.* Their author, the writer Arthur Holitscher, described his trip through the United States and Canada with appreciation for both countries and a compassionate understanding of their social ills. The articles so aroused Kafka's enthusiasm that he read them aloud to others and borrowed from them important details and overall impressions for his novel. It seems as if these articles (shortly thereafter edited as a book) and Benjamin Franklin's autobiography were the main sources of the novel later to be given by Brod the uninspiring and unfitting title *Amerika.*

The very first sentence, long, rhythmically beautiful, saying and implying much, makes it clear that this America will not be the land of red and white sons of nature:

As Karl Rossmann, a boy of sixteen who had been packed off to America by his impecunious parents because a servant girl had seduced him and got herself a child by him, stood on the liner slowly entering the harbour of New York, a sudden burst of sunshine seemed to illumine the Statue of Liberty, so that he saw it in a new light, although he had sighted it long before.[78]

It was fear of alimony payments and parental indignation, a common European mixture of economics and morality, that made Karl's parents send their young son to America. From the very beginning, the justice of their action is doubtful, and the doubts are increased as Karl's character begins to unfold.

The sight of the statue occupies the sensitive boy for quite a while, not only as a tourist attraction, but as an inner experience. As the other passengers begin to think of disembarking, he remains awed by the divine apparition in the increasingly stronger light: "The arm with the sword rose up as if newly stretched aloft, and round the figure blew the free winds of heaven. 'So high!' he said to himself, and was gradually edged to the very rail by the swelling throng of porters pushing past him, since he was not thinking at all of getting off the ship."[79]

The sword, neither a symbol of something frightful nor a criticism of America, as is often assumed, constitutes the first of the novel's many factual errors, sometimes comical to the initiated, but not basically harmful to the work. Thinking that he knew enough cultural details, Kafka informed his publisher with self-assurance that he "had represented the most modern New York." The sword held high is probably the impression he received from contemporary photographs taken from a considerable distance and blurring all details. The only colossal statue Kafka, the *Gymnasium* student, knew well, was the Hermann monument presenting this Germanic chief wielding his sword high above the Teutoburg Forest in which he had stopped the march of the Romans to the northern Germanic territories.

After the worship of the "mother of exiles," Karl's disembarkation is delayed by his forgotten umbrella. Returning to the interior of the ship in order to look for it, he mistakenly enters the cabin of a rough but good-natured stoker. The man tells him of his undeserved dismissal by a Rumanian foreman who disliked him because he was the only German in an otherwise Rumanian team. Convinced of the poor man's innocence, Karl accompanies him to the office of the captain, where he eagerly pleads the stoker's case before the officers and officials, only to be frustrated by the clumsiness of his "client."

That the stoker would lose his case was symbolically indicated by his attempt to kill a rat on the way to the captain's office. His awkward kick only helped it to slip faster into its hole, just as his awkward accusations against the "rat" Schubal helped his enemy to slip away from him. Kafka's subtle way of expressing his opinion, sometimes through traditional symbols rather than as narrator, is not sufficiently recognized by many critics who refuse to see anything traditional or literary in their author's work but discern only "revelations." Thus it could happen that the stoker's kick at the rat was interpreted as a sign of his brutality.[80] Or was it so long ago that sailors waged unrelenting war with the unrelenting rats on their ships?

As Karl mulls over in his mind a second plea, the one civilian in the office reveals himself to be his uncle, informed of his misfortune and exile to America by the maid who was the cause of it. This uncle, a tremendously rich businessman and senator, tells those present what he thinks of the contemptible way in which his nephew was treated. In spite of the abrupt and fortunate change in his situation, Karl continues to defend his helpless friend. But Senator Jacob, as the uncle is called in America, orders him to abandon his attempt, since they have all had enough, and more than enough, of the stoker. The nephew answers from a standpoint morally superior to that of his uncle: "But that's not the point in a question of justice."[81] The uncle, however, insists that they must go, and a sailor takes them to a waiting boat, Karl grieving so much for his abandoned friend that he bursts into tears. In the boat he looks at his protector, obviously influential enough to let him skip Ellis Island, and begins to doubt that this great man would ever be able to take the place of the humble stoker in his life.

Senator Jacob accepts Karl as a family member to be prepared for a brilliant career in his own business, a commission and dis-

patch agency of gigantic proportions. He introduces him to business friends, the banker Pollunder, the businessman Green, and
also to Mack, Pollunder's future son-in-law, who will help Karl
with compulsory riding lessons every morning at 5:30.

Mr. Pollunder is fond of Karl and asks him to visit him and
his daughter at their country home outside New York. Senator
Jacob does not like the idea of interrupting the training routine
of his nephew and only grudgingly gives him permission to stay
away for one evening. During the car ride to the country home
of Mr. Pollunder, Karl experiences the happiest hours in America
so far: "But Karl merely leaned back happily on the arm which
Mr. Pollunder had put around him; the knowledge that he would
soon be a welcome guest in a well-lighted country house surrounded by high walls and guarded by watch-dogs filled him
with extravagant well-being...."[82]

This feeling of being sheltered assumes an almost religious
significance in Kafka's life and work. He uses the same travel
metaphor with strong religious overtones ten years later:

... dann wirst du auch die unveränderliche dunkle Ferne sehn, aus
der nichts kommen kann als eben nur einmal ein Wagen, er rollt
heran, wird immer grösser, wird in dem Augenblick, in dem er bei
dir eintrifft, welterfüllend und du versinkst in ihm wie ein Kind in
den Polstern eines Reisewagens, der durch Sturm und Nacht fährt.[83]

... then you will also see the immutable dark distance out of which
there can come nothing but, sometime, that very carriage, bowling
nearer, growing ever larger, filling the whole world in the instant
when it draws level with you, and you will sink into it like a child
among the cushions of a travelling coach driving through the storm
and the night.[84]

Kafka's style has musical qualities although music did not interest
him. There is a crescendo in the short sentences: *er rollt heran,*
wird immer grösser, leading to a climax in the heavily stressed
words: *eintrifft, welterfüllend,* and a dying away in the concluding sentences with their gentle stresses. *Die dunkle Ferne*
which confronts the anxious man, to whom the inner voice speaks,

is still there as *Sturm und Nacht*, but now he is protected like a child in *den Polstern eines Reisewagens.*

The visit to the country home turns into the very opposite of all that Karl had anticipated while daydreaming in Mr. Pollunder's car. Mr. Green has been sent by the uncle to join the party, and this fat colossus turns out to be Karl's vicious enemy, against whom Mr. Pollunder, good-natured but weak, cannot protect his young friend. Green spoils Karl's dinner with his poor eating habits, and when Pollunder's daughter invites Karl to her room, the nervous boy is angered by her domineering manners. She throws him in a wrestling-match which she provokes and threatens to slap the face of "the welcome guest."

As an obedient nephew, Karl tries to leave early, but Mr. Green prevents it. The "illuminated" country home is a luxurious, enormous structure, but since it is being renovated it has electric light only in the dining room. Through one of the long dark corridors Karl sees, at the stroke of midnight, Mr. Green, candle in hand, swaying toward him, to surrender a letter written by his uncle and to be delivered at midnight. While Green holds the candle, Karl reads his uncle's condemning judgment: "Against my wishes you decided this evening to leave me; stick, then, to that decision all your life."[85]

The letter forbids Karl further communication with the uncle, but suggests that he accept Mr. Green's help and advice "during his first independent steps." Mr. Green's help consists merely in giving Karl a third-class ticket to San Francisco, and his advice is: to work his way up from the bottom. The perplexed boy says reproachfully to his enemy: "Does not the inscription quite plainly convey that midnight was to be the final term for me? And it is you who are to blame that I missed it."[86] Green's only answer is: "Not another word," and with that the "surrounding walls" disappear as he shoves Karl through a door. No longer "guarded by dogs" whose barking he hears on all sides, but in fear of them, the boy walks through the garden and reaches the highway to start marching along without knowing in what direction.

Green's last actions are contrary to his friend's wishes and should suffice to settle the most recent argument among critics[87] that Karl only "imagines" Green to be his brutal enemy. These

critics see no other meaning in the sharp cuts with which Green
dismembers the pigeon on his plate, but the correct way of
eating such a bird. However, in the traditional symbol language
of literature this pigeon is the helpless innocent Karl being
finished off brutally but adroitly by his immensely superior
opponent.

In the inn where he spends the rest of this calamitous night,
Karl meets Robinson and Delamarche, two unemployed metal
fitters, now tramps, who take him along to Ramses, a large town
in Kafka's America. Since they cheat him, abusing his naiveté,
Karl leaves them when offered a job as lift boy in the large
hotel *Occidental* near Ramses.

The completely drunk tramp Robinson is sent by Delamarche
to visit Karl at work and arouses the indignation of the head
waiter, who then fires the innocent lift boy without listening to
his explanation. Tearing himself loose from the sadistic porter
who wants to beat him severely, Karl loses his jacket, escaping
without money, papers, or suitcase. As a penniless vagrant fleeing
arrest by the police, he is practically kidnapped by Delamarche,
who forces him to be, together with Robinson, a servant to
himself and his enormously fat mistress Brunelda, a neurotic
former opera singer, all living together in one filthy little room.

Here the continuity of the narrative stops. A short fragment
presupposes that Brunelda has been left by Delamarche and
Robinson. Only Karl has remained, and he transports her in a
wheelchair to a brothel, "establishment No. 25," where he is
employed as errand boy. Without money or papers he has
apparently arrived at the lowest point in his life.

The first article exclusively dedicated to the structure of
Amerika stems from an adherent of the psychoanalytical school
whose main contributions to Kafka criticism appeared between
the thirties and fifties. The author begins with an informative
report on similarities between Dickens' works and Kafka's novel
and then gives psychoanalytical explanations like the following:
"Thus Karl sleeps out on the balcony with the passive Robinson
while Delamarche revels inside on the parental bed. Yet all three
are after the same object—the singer Brunelda whom Karl considers repulsive on the conscious level, but whom he finally treats
with loving care. Perhaps it is even relevant that Karl moves

with Brunelda to a cleaner apartment, once the mechanics are gone, away from the stale and filthy room where, like Kafka before him, he was so patently stuck fast in his 'original shapeless pulp.' "[88] But Delamarche is not after Brunelda, he possesses her; and it was possession at first glance. The "cleaner apartment" is a "greasy and repulsive" whorehouse in which Brunelda and Karl are going to work, Karl as an errand boy.

The following quotations are not maliciously chosen; they are typical of the errors Kafka critics who concentrate on psychoanalytic method commit over and over again. They do not read the text carefully, ignore or do not know the cultural backgrounds presented, and rely on translations without comparing them with the originals. The author quoted even forgets that Kafka wrote in German when he says: "There he [Karl] meets a stoker, and the very name suggests a source of life and power."[89] Disregarding the intentions of the author, such critics monotonously present their pansexual interpretation of human relations. On the photograph of Karl's parents, for example, "his small father stood very erect behind his mother."[90] Kafka lets us see the little man, conscious of his smallness, and makes us understand that he is compensating for it by the severity with which he has punished his son. The term "very erect" induces the critic to note: "What these images suggest is borne out in the novel: His [Karl's] repulsion for sex is rooted in his love for his mother; his insecurity, in his father's sharp disapproval and his phallic power; his later disillusionment, in the mother's basic loyalty to her husband."[91] Such remarks lead away from the novel to the well-trodden Oedipal path.

More essential than Karl's sexual problems are those concerning his existence in his new world. Most critics believe that he was intended to be one of the many who disappear in America and are *verschollen* ("never heard of again"). A minority is convinced that at the end of the novel, as Brod reports it, Karl will find a new home, work, dignity, in short, that he will be accepted.

VII   *Accepted*

How Karl freed himself from his last jobs in "offices," each of which seems to have been located "in a narrow dark alley,"

remains untold. Brod gave the last chapter the title "Das Naturtheater von Oklahoma" ("The Outdoor Theater of Oklahoma").
At the beginning of the chapter, Karl lives far from that state,
most likely in San Francisco, judging by the duration of the
train ride to Oklahoma and the description of the mountain
landscape through which he is traveling east. He might have
accepted Mr. Green's advice that his chances of earning a living
were best in San Francisco, where he would also be farthest
removed from the influence of his uncle.

At a street corner of San Francisco, or wherever Karl lives
at the beginning of the chapter, he sees a poster with the
following announcement:

The Oklahoma Theatre will engage members for its company today
at Clayton race-course from six o'clock in the morning until midnight.
The great Theatre of Oklahoma calls you! Today only and never
again! If you miss your chance now you miss it for ever! If you think
of your future you are one of us! Everyone is welcome! . . . But hurry,
so that you get in before midnight! At twelve o'clock the doors will
be shut and never opened again![92]

Again Kafka's otherwise realistic story takes on a strange mood.
The poster is a mixture of American high-powered advertising
and fairy-tale promises. The mysterious midnight hour had been
Karl's last chance before, when, at the stroke of twelve, the
prince suddenly became a pauper again. This time he is not
going to miss his chance. The phrase "Everybody is welcome" is
a mighty promise:

All that he had done till now was ignored; it was not going to be
made a reproach to him. He was entitled to apply for a job of which
he need not be ashamed. . . . He asked for nothing better; he wanted
to find some way of at least beginning a decent life, and perhaps
this was his chance.[93]

In order to be accepted by that mysterious but magnanimous
theater enterprise, those interested must go to Clayton, presumably of the fifteen American Claytons the one which is
located about twenty-five miles from San Francisco. With just
enough money for the fare he takes one of the subway trains

which connect many cities in Kafka's America. As he leaves the
station in Clayton, he is greeted by "the noise of many trumpets"
blown by hundreds of women who, dressed like angels, stand
on pedestals. One of them, a certain Fanny, explains to him
that every two hours they are relieved by as many trumpet-
blowing and drumming men dressed like devils. Fanny is not
mentioned in the previous chapters, but judging by the joy she
shows on seeing Karl, she must have played a role in Kafka's
plans for filling the gap before the last chapter.

The angels and devils seem to indicate that Kafka thought
of his theater in Oklahoma as one performing in the manner
in which medieval mystery plays were staged, spectacles performed outdoors for several days by hundreds of actors and
supers, many craftsmen, stage hands, etc. But did Kafka think
of such a theater? He always refers simply to the theater of,
or in, Oklahoma. The mellifluous name Oklahoma, which he
consistently misspelled Oklahama, seems to have attracted him,
but he never uses the term *Naturtheater* ("outdoor theater,"
"open-air theater"), which Brod had added as chapter heading.
In July, 1912, during his Goethe pilgrimage Kafka had visited
the miniature *Naturtheater* belonging to the summer castle
Belvedere, near Weimar, and knew, of course, the outdoor theaters in Germany which, in his time, were still few in number.
But although these modern theaters had a greater seating capacity
than ordinary theaters, they were far from colossal.

The hundreds of angels and devils in Clayton were supposed
to indicate the tremendous size of the Oklahoma theater, the
biggest in the world. Having walked through these throngs, the
people wanting to join are sent to very specialized offices. Karl,
for example, must go to a small building with the inscription:
European *Mittelschüler* ("lower grade secondary-school students")—he had complained to Mr. Pollunder about the four
lost years in a *Gymnasium*. After a short, more than lenient
interrogation, he informs the officials that he once thought of
becoming an engineer. Still embarrassed about his recent life,
he tells them that his name is Negro, a name the *déclassé* boy
was given in his last dishonorable position. The officials are
bewildered, but he is accepted and at once classified as a
technical worker.

The company invites the new members to an excellent turkey meal whose excellence is further proof that the theater is authentic, an unimpaired piece of reality, since excellent food has that meaning in Kafka's symbol language, just as, for instance, the filthy breakfast in Brunelda's room, scraped together from dirty dishes, characterizes the unreality of her accursed world.

In order to give the new members a first idea of the theater, a pack of photographs is passed around, but Kafka almost teasingly allows Karl, and therewith the reader, to see only the one which shows the president's box, all the others having been returned by the time Karl arrives at his place at the table. This presidential box is much larger than any of the imperial and royal boxes which exist in European theaters and opera houses, but it is built in the same neobaroque style, with a gilded curved balustrade, huge red velvet drapes, and subtle lighting effects, all of which makes such a box as unlikely a part of an outdoor theater as Fanny's remark: "It's an old theater, but it is always being enlarged."[94] Brod's use of the term *Naturtheater* as a chapter heading is poorly chosen, but it would have been only a slight mistake had not the impossible English translation "nature theater" in books and articles spawned useless commentaries. Even though the reader cannot imagine "this almost boundless theater" as an edifice in an American city, he is shown its benign influence on Karl's life, even in far-away Clayton. After he has met Fanny again, Karl meets, to his surprise and joy, young Giacomo who had introduced him to his duties in the Hotel Occidental. Thus rejoined with two people of his past whom he is delighted to see again, Karl begins to feel less lonely.

The last time we see Karl, he and Giacomo are on the train to Oklahoma City, looking out of the window of the railroad coach, admiring a high mountain range they are crossing. Karl seems to have forgotten all his sufferings and humiliations; he does not worry about what lies ahead, although, in the opinion of most critics, he rides to Oklahoma only to be killed there by his author.

According to Brod, and for literary reasons, it must be assumed that Kafka had a different end in mind. Brod reports in an epilogue to the novel that

It [the novel] remained unfinished. From what he told me I know
that the incomplete chapter about the Nature Theatre of Oklahoma
(a chapter the beginning of which particularly delighted Kafka, so
that he used to read it aloud with great effect) was intended to be
the concluding chapter of the work and should end on a note of
reconciliation. In enigmatic language Kafka used to hint smilingly,
that within this "almost limitless" theatre his young hero was going
to find again a profession, a stand-by, his freedom, even his old
home and his parents, as if by a charm of paradise.[95]

The absence of all these blessings was felt by Kafka as the tragedy
of his existence. All through his diaries there appear laments
about his unloved profession, his lack of freedom, about his
"Heimat" ("native city") Prague, the lack of support he hoped
in vain he might find in a wife. Only the desired reconciliation
with his parents was achieved, and that in the last months of
his fatal disease.

Without doubting Brod's credibility, critics, especially the
recent ones, argue that Kafka had planned a tragic end for his
novel. In 1965 and 1966 there appeared two lengthy books about
Amerika. Their authors,[96] like many others, insist that Karl's
train ride, which he begins with a jubilant heart, will be his
last one. They support their arguments with a remark made by
Kafka, and with references to the novel's structure.

Kafka wrote in September, 1915, in his diary: "Rossmann and
K. [the hero of *Der Prozess*], the innocent and the guilty, both
destroyed without distinction in the end, the guiltless one with
a gentler hand, more pushed aside than struck down."[97] This
passage settled for many critics the argument as to Karl's fate,
but it raises some serious doubts. First of all, the author does
not pronounce the death penalty in Karl's case, as some critics
ardently demand. The German word *umgebracht* has the double
meaning "killed" and "destroyed." A day before he wrote this
passage Kafka had used the same word about himself: "At one
time I used to think: Nothing will destroy you, not this tough,
clear, really empty head. . . ."[98] Also in this context *umbringen*
means "destroy," "ruin," definitely not "kill." What is more
important, the critics who demand Karl's death forget that Kafka
did not speak about his novel's last chapter but about the end
of the fragment as it existed in 1915. In that end Karl is not

"struck down," but "pushed aside." Running errands for a brothel, the boy who was a rich man's nephew being trained to become the rich man's successor is indeed ruined, destroyed (*umge-bracht*). After this temporary end of the novel, the author wrote later, in 1916, a last chapter which should leave no doubt that Karl is to rise again to a truly human level.

When Kafka made the grim diary entry about his hero's fate, he was deeply unhappy because of the broken engagement to Felice. In such moods he usually intensified his unhappiness with masochistic phantasies, and in this case he gloated over the fate of Karl and Joseph K., especially Karl, with whom he could identify himself, as with all his heroes. In 1912 he had written to Felice that he had sobbed so loudly while reading a passage in his novel concerning Karl that he was afraid of having awakened his parents; and again in 1913 he assured her: "The novel is me, my stories are me."[99]

In the beginning of 1915, months before he referred to Karl's destruction in "establishment No. 25," he thought of his hero in the spirit of the Oklahoma chapter which he had left un-finished but took up again in 1916: "I write my *Bouvard et Pécuchet* prematurely. If the two elements—most pronounced in "The Stoker" and "In the Penal Colony"—do not combine, I am finished. But is there any prospect of their combining?"[100] The elements he speaks of are represented in Flaubert's novel by the two title heroes. Bouvard has great hopes for the future of mankind while his friend Pécuchet sees its end in final anarchy. This passage indicates that Kafka saw his novel as an optimistic work; there is hope for a young courageous man like Karl. In "Die Strafkolonie," however, he is deeply pessimistic, indicating first signs of a developing anarchy of values.

In 1916 Kafka turned once more toward the Oklahoma chapter. How much he added to it is uncertain. At any rate, he finished it, if only by setting off two paragraphs which once were its unfinished end as the beginning of a new chapter. The first part of the Oklahoma chapter ended with the American lads sitting opposite Karl and Giacomo laughing at the enthusiasm of these two foreigners. To this Kafka added in 1916 a few lines about insensitive, smooth American faces which once he had so en-thusiastically praised.

There are also literary reasons why one might assume that the hero of *Amerika* was to rise again after his deep fall. Critics maintain that after the lowest point in his career Karl can only descend to death, but for that very reason he might also rise again as the structure of stories with two climaxes shows. In his self-belittling way, Kafka had said that his novel was nothing but an imitation of Dickens, and there are similarities between his *Amerika* and *David Copperfield* and *Oliver Twist*. Structurally, Kafka's novel resembles *Oliver Twist*. Both works belong to a story type which, like the Joseph story in the Old Testament, has two climaxes in the hero's fortunes, both preceded by a fall. Oliver Twist suffers in a workhouse, in the undertaker's place, and in the den of thieves, but is saved by the rich and kindhearted Mr. Brownlow. He is kidnapped and returned to the den of thieves but freed after a short captivity; and in the end Mr. Brownlow adopts him. Karl's first period of suffering is shorter: After a few months of parental rage and a steerage voyage into exile, his rich uncle, Senator Jacob, takes him into his house. After two and a half months of happiness his uncle casts him out forever. He works hard as a liftboy for another two months, is kept prisoner by two criminals, and after that, penniless and without papers, finds work only in the social netherworld. The Oklahoma chapter was to bring the second, in this case near miraculous, elevation to the high state of a meaningful, perhaps even happy, existence.

A mood as in a fairy tale approaching its happy end, and then again almost religious emotions, prevail throughout this penultimate chapter and the two paragraphs of the last one. They were all inspired, as Brod suggested and a modern critic explained,[101] by Arthur Holitscher's article about Canada (1912) and his book *Amerika heute und morgen* (America Today and Tomorrow, 1912). Holitscher described the joys and hopes of poor Europeans accepted by immigration officials as settlers in the wide expanses of arable land in underpopulated Canada. Speaking of the poor and defeated coming to the New World, he uses religious terminology: "This country Canada . . . now one begins to feel what it is—Canaan. It has space and bread and hope for a hundred million people. Here is immediate help for the hungry ones, the unemployed, the rejected. . . ."[102] Holitscher describes how he remained in the Winnipeg railroad station all day watching the joy of the poor, the men chased away and mocked in the old country.

This enthusiasm animated the Oklahoma chapters. Karl is no longer *der Verschollene* ("the man who was never heard of again"). Many critics have adopted this title instead of Brod's colorless *Amerika*. By using it they wanted to indicate that they believed in a tragic ending of the novel. Kafka, who himself had used it twice, the last time in 1914, never used it again, probably because it contradicted his new intentions as he last worked on the Oklahoma chapters in 1916.

The strange Oklahoma theater of wish fulfillment is typically American in its advertising methods and colossal size. But it also belongs to another realm where paradise, the grail for which a pure fool like Karl quests, and similar dreams of salvation come from. Perhaps the outdoor theater anticipates something more real: Palestine, where every exiled Jew was welcome, and where there was a homeland without quotation marks.

CHAPTER 5

Punishments

I *The Trial of Franz Kafka*

FROM August to December, 1914, Kafka wrote, if not all, then by far the greatest part of his novel *Der Prozess* (*The Trial*) whose basic metaphor is also its title. *Der Prozess* had forerunners in Kafka's writings. The greater part of "Das Urteil" was the trial of a son before a father-judge who pronounced the death penalty for the accused. In *Amerika* the stoker was on trial, defended by the hero, who later had to face unfair judges before the "hotel tribunal."

The frequent use of the trial motif is much more indicative of Kafka's inner life than of his law studies; he himself was continuously on trial before his own guilt feelings which, he was convinced, had been shaped in early youth by his father's tyrannical behavior. The real source of his novel can be found in the *Letter*: "I had lost my self-confidence where you were concerned, and in its place had developed a boundless sense of guilt. (In recollection of this boundlessness I once wrote of someone, accurately: 'He is afraid the shame will outlive him, even.')"[1] These are the last feelings of Joseph K., the hero of *Der Prozess*, dying by the hands of his executioners.

In the same *Letter*, Kafka uses the term "trial" as a metaphor, speaking of himself and Ottla engaged in a "terrible trial that is pending between us and you, ... a trial in which you keep on claiming to be the judge, whereas ... you are a party too, just as weak and deluded as we are."[2]

Passages anticipating, or varying, motifs that occur in *Der Prozess* also appear long before, during, and after Kafka's work on that novel. There are contemptuous descriptions of his own character, guilt feelings, self-condemnations, invocations of punishments, phantasies of being tortured or cruelly executed. In

89

December, 1910, three and a half years before Kafka started the novel, he spoke with the eloquence of a prosecuting attorney about his own "misdeeds" committed on a level which concerns neither state nor church, nor the ordinary conscience, but only an extremely refined and implacable critical sense: "How do I excuse yesterday's remark about Goethe (which is almost as untrue as the feeling it describes...)? In no way. How do I excuse my not yet having written anything today? In no way.... I have continually an invocation in my ear: 'If you would only come, invisible tribunal.' "[3] This is the first mention of a court, comparable to the secret legal organization of the novel. What Kafka expected from this tribunal he says repeatedly, as, for example, in 1911 when he wished for a death penalty as described in the novel: "This morning, for the first time in a long time, the joy again of imagining a knife twisted in my heart."[4]

Kafka's self-accusations became most intense when he broke his first engagement to Felice. Very early, at the end of the first year of this struggle that was to last five years, he realized that he tortured her, and yet he continued to write to her. After short intervals he would resume the protracted torment because he needed and craved her letters like an addict.

In the twenty months between the completion of "Die Verwandlung" and the beginning of his next creative period, when work on *Der Prozess* was proceeding well, Kafka wrote to Felice what amounts to some 400 closely printed pages. Not love as passion or tenderness drove him, but his craving for this unreal form of feminine interest and his need of merely talking to an understanding woman. His correspondence with Grete Bloch from November, 1913, to early July, 1914, had similar reasons since he also solicited of her more correspondence than her role as an intermediary required. With these letters, more than 530 pages in print, he urged the two young women to write to him frequently, but the price came high: for a year and a half, Kafka, the writer, lacked all creative energy.

As the approaching first engagement made him realize that marriage threatened his dream world, he was horrified and overcome by feelings of guilt. He felt accused and expressed this feeling in metaphors taken from the world of criminal trials: police arrests, and even executions. As happened on other oc-

casions, the still unwritten work of which he had not even
thought announced itself in his choice of metaphors and similes.
During the engagement ceremony he felt only guilt and shame.
Five days later he described his role during this traditional
occasion: "Was tied hand and foot like a criminal. Had they
sat me down in a corner bound in real chains, placed policemen
in front of me, . . . it could not have been worse."[5] The disengagement taking place six weeks later in a Berlin hotel inspired a
diary entry couched in similar style. Under the heading "The
tribunal in the hotel" Kafka, the judge, declares Kafka, the
culprit, to be "devilish in all innocence."[6] The next day he sent
to Felice's parents a farewell letter, which he called "a speech
from the place of execution."

After having faced the tribunal, he went to a restaurant with
Erika, Felice's sister, who liked him as much as she felt sorry
for Felice. Erika tried to console him, although she had seen
him accused "at court."

His feeling of having wronged Felice was predominant when
he wrote *Der Prozess*; yet guilt was essentially not caused by
this or that particular action, but by his view of himself as a
flawed human being. There is no doubt that he was dissatisfied
with himself, but some of his more violent confessions also leave
no doubt that he was overwhelmed by the feeling of the moment,
exaggerating his flaws in passionate yet well-chosen words.

Still depressed by his first disengagement, his self-hatred bursts
out: I am "full of lies, hate, and envy.—Full of incompetence,
stupidity, thickheadedness.—Full of laziness, weakness, and helplessness. Thirty-one years old."[7] The dashes are added by the
author to stress Kafka's rhetorical figure, the triadic arrangement.
Three groups of three flaws each give the sentence rhythm
and emphasize its content. It seems as if, unconsciously, Kafka's
feeling for style had intensified this moral self-analysis. How
else could he have accused himself of "inability, stupidity, obtuse-
ness," characteristics which he did not possess, no matter how
severe the criteria applied might be. The evidence of his writing
and all that is known about him contradict this self-accusation.

He himself seems to have known that the purpose of such
exaggerations, particularly in his letters to women, was questionable, and repeatedly called himself a liar. But no matter how

exaggerated the above enumeration of flaws might have been, he was sincere in his praise of the simple, authentic life with which he balances the diatribe against himself in the same passage:

I saw the two agriculturists in Ottla's picture. Young, fresh people possessed of some knowledge and strong enough to put it to use among people who in the nature of things resist their efforts somewhat. One of them leading beautiful horses; the other lies in the grass, the tip of his tongue playing between his lips in his otherwise unmoving and absolutely trustworthy face.[8]

Kafka liked to contrast himself, as well as some of the defeated heroes of his stories, with representatives of an unbroken existence, as, for example, in "Die Verwandlung," where Grete is so contrasted to her brother Gregor.

The sins of which Kafka accuses himself all stem from what he called his *Beziehungslosigkeit zum Leben,* his not being committed to life. Shortly after he had started work on his novel, he exclaimed: "My monotonous, empty, mad bachelor's life!"[9] It was the main lament about his life, or, better, the main self-accusation often expressed before, and to be repeated frequently.

A few months after tuberculosis had cruelly interrupted the monotony of his existence, and long after he had laid aside *Der Prozess,* doomed to remain a fragment, Kafka wrote a contemplative letter to Brod. In part it reads like a commentary on his novel, to which it refers with the same quotation he had used in the *Letter:* "In the city, in the family, in my profession, in society, in the love relation (put it first, if you wish), in the existing community of our people, or the one we are striving for, in all of this I did not stand the test...." He sums up: "A miserable life, a miserable death, 'It was as if the shame were to survive him' is more or less the final word of the trial novel."[10]

II   *The Arrest of Joseph K.*

"The tribunal in the hotel" may have been the germinal metaphor for the Secret Law Court of *Der Prozess* or at least for its venue in an even less dignified place—on the fifth floor of a tenement house, inhabited by members of the poorest class.

Its offices, at least those which concern Joseph K., the hero of the novel, are in the attic above; but as he is to find out later. "Law Court offices are in almost any attic." The air in these attics is as hot and unbreathable as it was in the hotel to which Kafka returned after his "trial," as he described it on July 23. Six days later, the name Joseph K. appears in a short paragraph, followed by others, all beginnings of stories which break off after a few lines. But Kafka did not give up; he wrote *Der Prozess*, which he never completely finished, but which is not as fragmentary as *Amerika*.

The protagonist Joseph K., the only son of a widowed mother, has made a successful career for himself in a large bank where, as chief clerk, he has only the director and the assistant manager as his superiors. On his thirtieth birthday, his ordinary life ends because, on the morning of that day, strangers, an Inspector and two guards, appear in the boarding house where he has rented a room, telling the surprised young man, who is not aware of having done anything wrong, that he is under arrest.

The two guards, obviously bribable fellows, appropriate his underwear and even his breakfast, maintaining that the underwear will be safer with them than in the corrupt depot. The Inspector, with rude indifference to the privacy of the innocent, has settled in the apartment of another roomer, a Miss Bürstner, who has already left for work. Facing the Inspector after he has been urged to put on his best suit, the bewildered Joseph K. wants to call up the highest-ranking among his friends, the widely respected prosecuting attorney Hasterer. It seems to be the normal thing to do even in these strange circumstances, and he is readily granted the permission by the Inspector supervising his arrest. But the permission is accompanied by the strange remark: "But I don't see what sense there would be in that, unless you have some private business to consult him about."[11] K. is completely bewildered since there is no connection between the ordinary court system of the land and the mysterious Court whose lowliest emissaries he is dealing with, but he is not left completely uninformed. Vulgar and corrupt though the guards are, and in spite of the noncommittal attitude of the Inspector, K. receives some information about the institution which has sent them. As one of the guards explains: "We're quite capable of grasping the fact that the high authorities we serve, ... must be quite well informed about the reasons for the arrest and the person of the prisoner."[12] That the actions of these authorities are expressions of K.'s inner states and not actions in the real world is clearly hinted at in another statement of the guards, one of the most revealing in the entire novel: "Our officials never go hunting for guilt in the populace, but, as the Law decrees, are attracted by guilt, and must then send out us warders."[13] The guilt attracts or brings out self-accusations and self-condemnations once the guilty one becomes aware of being guilty, even if he cannot name his guilt; and so his inner trial begins.

When K. protests that he does not know the law which he is supposed to have broken, the other guard remarks to his comrade: "He admits that he doesn't know the Law and yet he claims he's innocent."[14] The Inspector advises K. to "think less about us and of what is going to happen to you, think more about yourself instead. And don't make such an outcry about your feeling innocent."[15]

From all the novel reveals, it is clear that K.'s guilt is not related to a crime or other offense which concerns ordinary law courts. Until shortly before his gruesome death, the accused hero does not have a clear understanding of what he is guilty of, but Kafka sees to it that the reader does. He does so in an important passage which follows immediately upon the end of the scene depicting the strange arrest, as if it were to justify that scene, however disconnected from it the passage may appear at first reading. Not only its position within the novel but also the style in which it is rendered call for the reader's special attention. Breaking with his usual restriction to the perspective of the hero, the author seems to interrupt the flow of the narrative, steps onto the proscenium, and reports:

That spring K. had been accustomed to pass his evenings in this way: after work whenever possible—he was usually in his office until nine—he would take a short walk, alone or with some of his colleagues, and then go to a beer hall, where until eleven he sat at a table patronized mostly by elderly men. But there were exceptions to this routine, when, for instance, the Manager of the Bank, who highly valued his diligence and reliability, invited him for a drive or for dinner at his villa. And once a week K. visited a girl called Elsa, who was on duty all night till early morning as a waitress in a cabaret and during the day received her visitors in bed.[16]

The sins of omission in this life are easily enumerated. It is devoid of love, removed from nature, not enriched by literature, the theater, books, or music. Even the busy official Kafka found time for reading, the theater, and even sports like swimming, rowing, and horseback riding. Most important, K. does not hunger for "the unknown food" like his nobler brother Gregor Samsa. How much better does Kafka's condemnation of his own life as "a monotonous, empty insane bachelor's life" fit that of Joseph K., for whom the cruel death penalty is decreed which the author joyfully imagined carried out on himself: "A knife twisted in the heart."

But in one point the author burdened K. with his own real guilt: in his relation to his mother. Many and variegated are the harsh criticisms of old Mrs. Kafka in her son's diary and his letters to Felice. Thus he confesses: "I have never found in any family, whether of friends or relations, as much coldness and false friendliness as I have always felt obliged to show toward my parents (through my fault as well as theirs)."[17] Unloving remarks about his mother's misunderstanding him and the world abound; there is even one about her body, misshapen by faulty diet and childbearing. K. has likewise no filial love for his mother and gives her nothing but financial support. In spite of her repeated wishes that he should come and visit her—since she is old and infirm and cannot travel to see him—he did not find the time to see her once in three years. Nor has he shown interest in any of those relatives who are concerned about him. When his cousin, an eighteen-year-old schoolgirl in K.'s town, whom he never contacts, tries to visit him in the bank, she is not permitted to disturb her busy relative.

Like Bendemann in "Das Urteil," K. also lacks the gift of being a good friend; he is not even a good companion to the "learned, respected, influential" gentlemen, mostly lawyers, at "the reserved table." He thinks, in the first place, how advantageous it is to be in a position to talk to such men, and, besides, that he could also establish "personal relations with the Court,

which were always useful."[18] The friendship offered him by
the Prosecuting Attorney Hasterer was, of course, highly welcome and K. cultivated it cleverly so that it became an intimate
friendship.

The secret Court which has initiated criminal proceedings
against K. is as real and as unreal as the beetle Gregor Samsa,
and is also closely fused with a realistically described environ-
ment, which is, in this case, a typical central European town
with elegant residential quarters, slums, night clubs, restaurants,
streetcars, and taxis. The giant metaphor "Secret Court" seems
to illustrate the trial in K.'s soul. His innermost feelings, which
are offended by the life he is leading and initially silenced,
repressed, and ridiculed by K.'s mind, win out in the end and
call forth in him a growing desire for purification through
punishment.

What we hear about the Court in the novel and what Kafka
reveals by his self-accusations, his phantastic descriptions of
punishments, and "the invisible Court," seems to make this
interpretation plausible. Once Kafka has created such a key
metaphor, he retains and develops it with ever new inventions
within its compass.

Joseph K. is not completely ignorant of his inner state. Guilt
feelings lie dormant in the bank official until on his thirtieth
birthday they awake faster than his conscious mind; and so he
is arrested, never to escape the power of his inner judges. Kafka
comes closest to indicating the nature of the Court in two
passages, one of which is crossed out. This passage, preserved
by the editor, Brod, seems to have been omitted by the author
since it contains an allusion to Proust, and Kafka habitually
avoided quotations or allusions to other writers. In this sup-
pressed passage, K. is told by someone "that when you wake up
in the morning you nearly always find everything in exactly the
same place as the evening before."[19] In Swann's Way, Proust's
narrator Marcel speaks of "the good angel of certainty"[20] who
keeps everything in place during the night. This good angel
had not protected K., who is further told by this someone that
"the moment of waking up was the riskiest moment of the day.
Once that was well over without deflecting you from your orbit,
you could take heart of grace for the rest of the day."[21] But K.

had been "pulled away" from his carefree existence to encounter mounting misgivings, sorrows, humiliations, and finally death. In the standard text, a similar idea is expressed. Mrs. Grubach, K.'s sympathizing landlady, has her own opinion about his arrest: "It gives me the feeling of something very learned . . . which I do not understand, but which there is no need to understand." K. regards her opinion as being in part correct and adds:

. . . I was taken by surprise, that was all. . . . In the Bank, for instance, I am always prepared, nothing of that kind could possibly happen to me there, I have my own attendant, the general telephone and the office telephone stand before me on my desk, people keep coming in to see me, clients and clerks, and above all, my mind is always on my work and so kept on the alert. . . .[22]

This last statement might be considered the key to the work. The mysterious Court is in his mind; it is a state of mind that K. never before allowed to gain dominance over his inner self.

In the very beginning, but even then with dubious success, K. tries to make light of his arrest, but when angered by the prudish gossip of his landlady about Miss Bürstner, in whose room he had to face the Inspector, he blurts out that he should be the first of the boarders to be given notice, if she was concerned for the purity of her boarding house. The concept of impurity as Kafka uses it does not refer primarily to K.'s affair with Elsa, the waitress. What he considers "impure" is, in the first place, an inner dishonesty, the hind thoughts, hidden motives with which modern man is beset. Kafka calls himself a representative of this type, "a rat's nest of miserable dissimulations . . . even the doubts self-scrutiny begets will soon grow weak and self-complacent as the wallowing of a pig in muck."[23]

This inner dishonesty is a characteristic of K. and he demonstrates it on the evening of his arrest in his attempt to gain Miss Bürstner's help. She feels the impure mixture of calculation and sexual hunger in him and refuses her help, for the time being at least.

In spite of K.'s mocking remarks in this first chapter, there are also ominous overtones, foreshadowing the tragic end. One of the guards speaks of K.'s "great accursed trial," and the idea of suicide comes fleetingly to the mind of the defendant.

Even more effective than such unmistakable hints is the hidden terror of the arrest scene which becomes more and more intense when the vulgar underlings treat K., a member of a bank triumvirate, like a convict or when the Inspector points out the futility of calling up an attorney. The mood of these scenes has induced some critics, including Brod, to assume that the clairvoyant Kafka anticipated the Nazi regime and the horror of Gestapo arrests. Since, as a schoolboy, Kafka had learned about the Vehmic Courts of the later Middle Ages, it seems more likely that the secret tribunals of that institution inspired him. Unexpectedly, their dreaded emissaries would appear in the guilty man's home or leave a message that he was summoned to appear before them. K.'s execution resembles the methods of the Vehmic Courts, which used to send three chosen men to overpower the condemned culprit and kill him at some secret spot.

III   *The Trial of Joseph K.*

Sunday is the day chosen by the Court for K.'s first interrogation, so that his professional work will not be disturbed by the appointment. Still considering his arrest ridiculous, he decides to attend, but then has great difficulty finding the courtroom in the huge apartment building full of poor people. He is finally directed by a pretty woman, who apparently lives there, since she is doing her washing in an adjacent room.

Disgusted by the shabby surroundings and contemptuous of the Examining Magistrate, who is so uninformed that he believes the defendant to be a house painter, K. delivers a lengthy harangue against this institution, its general inefficiency and dishonest underlings. He acknowledges the magnitude and complexity of the Court:

"There can be no doubt that . . . behind my arrest and today's interrogation, there is a great organization at work. An organization which not only employs corrupt warders, oafish Inspectors, and Examining Magistrates . . . but which also has at its disposal a judicial hierarchy of high, indeed of the highest rank, with an indispensable and numerous retinue of servants, clerks, police, and other assistants, perhaps even hangmen, I do not shrink from that word."[24]

In the midst of this otherwise hilarious scene ominous overtones again anticipate the tragic end.

While K. talks to his seemingly attentive listeners, he is interrupted by the lustful shrieks of a young man holding in tight embrace the pretty woman who had ushered him into the room, drawing the people's attention away from K., who then leaves. On the following Sunday, he returns to the room of his defeat, but is told, to his disappointment, that the court is not in session. His informant, again the pretty young woman, also tells him that the young man who had caused the commotion is a law student, but not in the academic sense, since he studies the jurisprudence practiced by the secret Court. Hesitantly she unlocks the empty room of the previous Sunday's session, and K. discovers on the desk of the Examining Magistrate two books; the one, according to its title, is the tale of a husband's sadistic treatment of his wife; the other, when opened by K., reveals an ineptly drawn pornographic illustration. He remarks: "These are the law books that are studied here. These are the men who are supposed to sit in judgment on me."[25]

The woman, the custodian's wife, begins to flirt with K., and when she begs to be taken away receives his ready promise. He sees in her a possible helper in his fight with the Court, just as he expected Miss Bürstner might be. His rising hopes are rudely crushed by the sudden appearance of the student, who carries the woman straight to the Examining Magistrate, her other lover. K.'s attempts to interfere are easily warded off by the surprisingly strong young go-between. It is the second time K. is defeated by the Court, and again in the field of sex, not of justice.

Immediately after the abduction of the custodian's wife, he meets her husband, who, as she says, is helpless against the rapacious court members and their generously practiced *droit de seigneur*. To satisfy his curiosity, K. accepts the unhappy cuckold's invitation to visit the Court offices in the attic and finds, as he had suspected, that the interior of this legal institution is as shabby as its exterior. Overcome by the extreme heat and the fetid air, K. has to be almost bodily carried out to recuperate.

Whenever Kafka lets his hero defy the Court, he employs motifs of a tradition satirizing judges and legal procedures, particularly the one representing the men of the law as great woman hunters. This motif antedates even the amorous Bolognese attorney Dr. Graziano of the *commedia dell' arte*. Numerous were the satires on the legal profession in the late nineteenth and early twentieth centuries, and not only in literature. There exists a painting by Jules Girardet which could almost serve as an illustration of the Court scene. It shows the presiding judge at a trial, smiling forlornly, while below his bench a wildly gesticulating attorney orates. Around the head of the judge flutter, airily painted, ballet danseuses with waving tutus—his daydream. And *Jurisprudence*, as depicted by the art nouveau painter Gustav Klimt, pictures octopuses holding naked women in sensual embraces. Whether Kafka knew any of these paintings is as uncertain as it is irrelevant; but he certainly knew the motif.

The metaphorical world of *Der Prozess* follows the highs and lows in K.'s inner life. Comical scenes are followed by serious ones, as far as the fragmentary character of the novel allows one to speak of its composition. The grotesquely amusing scenes in the tenement house should be followed by the chapter entitled *The Flogger*, demonstrating the archaic harshness of the mysterious Court. But Max Brod, the editor, put this chapter in the wrong place.

On hearing someone sigh in the lumber-room of the bank, K. enters to find behind a wall of old discarded papers and ink bottles a man who, in his outer appearance, seems to be a mixture of medieval executioner and a mate of the old British navy who knows how "to lay it on with a will." His two victims are the dishonest guards who arrested K. and now beg him to interfere. Helpless and frightened, K. flees when their punishment begins. Visiting the room again, late in the evening of the next day, he finds the scene unchanged, the culprits still asking for help. Almost crying, he runs to the bank employees who are still busy at their copying machines and orders them to clean up the lumber-room. They promise to do that—the next day. A flogger, beating the same victims a night and a day, and normal bank activities going on a few rooms away—that shows how closely, in his novel, Kafka fuses the world of his extended metaphors with the real world.

At a point in his trial when K. begins to show signs of the

loser's fatigue, his well-meaning uncle offers to take him for consultation to an old friend of his, the lawyer Huld. But in spite of Huld's many contacts with the legal personnel of the Secret Court, K. has no confidence in him. His mental reservation is: "But you're attached to the Court in the Palace of Justice, not to the one in the attics."[26]

It is at the bed of the ailing Huld that K. meets an important member of the Secret Court, its Chief Clerk; yet with incredible frivolity he leaves the room to join Leni, Huld's nurse and housekeeper, awaiting him in the seclusion of her employer's office. While amorously dallying with him, Leni reveals that she knows much about his trial, and the advice she offers him touches upon his real situation, his struggle against his better insight and his guilt feelings. She has heard that he is too unyielding and advises him now: "... you can't fight against this Court, you must confess to guilt. ... Until you do that, there's no possibility of getting out of their clutches, none at all. Yet even then you won't manage it without help from the outside, but you needn't trouble your head about that, I'll see to it myself."[27] While she seduces him and claims him as her lover, the infuriated uncle waits in the street to inform his nephew that the Chief Clerk of the Court, who is right now in charge of the criminal case of Joseph K., could not wait any longer and has left. Thus the defendant has deprived himself of his best chance to improve his position.

It soon becomes apparent to K. how little help he can expect from Lawyer Huld, whose descriptions of the Secret Court are a satire of officials in real courts. They are, as he states at length, careless, mean, dishonest, without contact with the people, secretive, continuously irritated, revengeful, sulky like children, and erratic. Only lawyers know how to deal with them, and even they fail at times. Of real value to a client is only his lawyer's honest, personal connection with higher officials of the lower ranks. Similar to Kafka's satire of lawyers, not in style, of course, but in content, is *Lesebuch für Angeklagte* (*A Reader for Defendants*) by a certain Walter Rode, published in 1931, which shows that conditions had not changed much after the First World War. One short example must suffice: "If the lawyer whom the defendant has chosen is not only known but also popular in

Court circles, then his client advances from a suspected stranger to a fellow club member. The Court, the unfriendly Bench, smiles when it sees him."[28]

Tiring of Huld, who talks in circles about the Court and how useful he is to his client, K. dismisses him and thus enters into a new phase of his relation to his trial. He no longer despises but rather respects the Secret Court; and although he does not believe in his guilt, he reconsiders the trial, which now appears to him as a "big business deal where a party had to hold fast to its own advantage." Planning to draw up a plea, he also plans a war of attrition against the officials. He himself, "or one of the women or some other messenger must keep at the officials day after day and force them ... to study his papers."[29] Among these women is Miss Bürstner, who was to have played an important role in parts of the novel he did not write since K. reflects that "his relations with Miss Bürstner seemed to fluctuate with the case itself."[30]

Looking around for new helpers, K. comes upon the painter Titorelli who is the Secret Court's portraitist, living in a stuffy attic, which turns out to be part of a loft where the Secret Court has offices. On the stairs to the painter's attic, he encounters a group of young girls who treat him with mockery, sensing his inner insecurity. "'These girls belong to the Court too,'" the painter whispers into K.'s ear and adds half in jest, half in explanation: "'You see, everything belongs to the Court.'"[31] Joseph K.'s insecure inner self continuously receives new judgments, new accusations from the outer world. In one of Kafka's long diary condemnations of the bachelor "without a center, a profession, a love, a family, a private income" there is a similar passage of self-condemnation induced by the attitude of outsiders: "Often you can already recognize yourself, if you pay attention, in the face of the servant at the door."[32]

Titorelli paints the lower judges in mighty poses since, according to him, the gentlemen are vain. The portrait he is working on during K.'s visit shows, as adornment of the judge's chair, a Justitia who also looks to K. like the goddess of the Hunt. Without knowing it, he has described his own situation, for he is being hunted down by the Court. The goddess of the Hunt may bring to the reader's mind the Erinyes, the unrelenting huntresses of the guilty, untouched by pleas and repentance, classical forerunners of Kafka's Secret Court.

Shortly afterward, he is asked by the bank's manager to show a visiting Italian client the local cathedral and its art treasures. Before he leaves on his assignment, Leni calls him up and, finding out where he is going, says pityingly: "They are hounding you," using a hunting metaphor, and K., who has recognized by now that he is the hunted, repeats: "Yes, they are hounding me." There is no Italian client in the building, but a priest telling him from the height of the pulpit that he, the prison chaplain, has summoned him to the cathedral. Being informed by the priest that his case is almost hopeless, his guilt considered proved in the lower Court, K. for the last time asserts his innocence and expresses a wish to look for new helpers. The priest disapproves, warning him especially against using women to intercede for him, but K. protests that women have much power, particularly in this Court, which consists, for the most part, of petticoat hunters. Angered by hearing the Court impugned, but also frightened for the defendant, the priest shouts at K.: "Why can't you see two steps ahead?"

Regretting his emotional outburst, the priest comes down from the pulpit to talk calmly with the guilty man. Still, although K. does not understand the priest, he hopes to receive advice from him, how to "circumvent it, break away from it, live outside of it." Starting this naive request with the revealing phrase: "With you I can be frank," he is stopped by the priest, who warns him that he is deluded in his ideas about the Court. To illustrate the delusion, the priest tells him a parable which K. had anticipated, in part, in his plans of "circumventing his case, breaking away from it altogether, [finding] a mode of living outside of the Jurisdiction of the Court." It is a mysterious parable which not even the prison chaplain's commentaries completely explain.

A man from the country arrives at the door which leads into the Law. Asking the big, ugly doorkeeper's permission to enter, he is told that he may not enter now, but perhaps later; should he try to go past him, he would find from hall to hall even more powerful and frightening doorkeepers. The man is baffled since the Law is supposed to be always accessible. He sits down on a stool near the entrance and waits for days and years, wearying the doorkeeper with his entreaties. He also tries to bribe him, and the doorkeeper accepts what he has to offer not as a bribe, but to give the poor man the feeling that he has tried everything. Growing old and childish, the petitioner even begs the fleas in the doorkeeper's fur collar to help him persuade the obstinate man.

In the end, the dying man sees the radiance of the law streaming through the door and asks the doorkeeper: "Everyone strives to attain the Law, how does it come about, then, that in all these years no one has come seeking admittance but me?" The doorkeeper bellows into his ear: "No one but you could gain admittance through this door, since this door was intended for you. I am now going to shut it."[33]

K. seeks justification, just as the man from the country wants to enter into the Law: both goals belong together, because K. wants to find out in what way he has broken the Law, which, as he confesses in the beginning, he does not know. Tenaciously both men, living "outside the Law," seek, by dubious and ineffective means, to achieve their supreme goals. Shortly after the cathedral scene K. is executed.

IV Joseph K. Is Not Everyman

The first detailed discussions of Der Prozess appeared in the first full-sized book about Kafka by a man of letters with strong psychoanalytic interests. The book appeared in 1947, in the decade fond of Kafka, Kierkegaard, and psychoanalytical amateurs. Its author comes to surprising apodictic results like the following: "Since it is indisputable that we have here [in Der Prozess], whatever else, a paranoic persecution with delusions of reference, it is necessary to look for the specific repressed homosexuality; and this is indicated by the fantasies of taking revenge against the Court by getting their women and offering his own. . . ."[34] Besides having "indisputable" arguments, the author asserts at one point that there is no alternative between his and some other method, but only between his method "and no interpretation at all."[35]

He interprets the execution of K. as a homosexual contest: "The two executioners come, 'pallid and plump with top-hats that were apparently incollapsible,' these plump ones are the infants, the hated brothers, and himself as the third infant [sic]."

"The hated brothers" died, the one six months old, the other a year and a half. The executioners' "incollapsible hats are the rival penises that will never wilt."[36] But their hats are in German called *unverrückbar* ("immovable"); these men are typical private "dicks" with their hard hats pulled onto their heads and seldom taken off. In the novel, K. cannot muster the courage to take the knife and kill himself. The German text reads: "Er konnte sich nicht bewähren" ("He could not do what was expected of him"). The critic translates, correctly in this case: "He could not rise to the occasion," which meets his interpretation: "His penis will not rise to the occasion, it will be a fiasco."[37]

This kind of criticism is practiced only by a few writers. To most of those commenting upon *Der Prozess* it seems obvious that its hero, Joseph K., as one critic puts it, "by remaining a nondescript Everyman, appears as universally typical."[38] Theological and existential interpretations are centered around key concepts like universal man, man's queries, man's guilt, and the condition of man and his sinful state, thus making the novel a modern story of Everyman.

How could the lonely bachelor K., living his confused, meaningless existence outside of the "Law," represent man and his relations to the absolute? It is not only his bachelorhood that sets him off from his fellow human beings; he is further limited by having characteristics he does not share with a vast majority of his fellow men in Prague or any other European city. As the author explicitly states, K. is a member of the educated middle class from which most of the accused stem; the so-called lower classes have other worries. Most important, he has a trial which further isolates him and almost makes him an outcast who wonders whether simple people will still shake hands with him. He belongs to a small minority compared with those whom the Secret Court has not accused and cannot accuse since they blithely agree with the law of church, state, or party and, if they are guilty, know very well what sin, crime, or offense they are guilty of. Even the priest in the novel insists, in the spirit of the Court he serves, on the difference between the guilty and the innocent.

If commentators speak of man's condition, they include, presumably, women, although in many cultures there exists a tendency to think primarily of males when generalizations about man are made. Kafka does not explicitly say that the accused are all men, but it would be hard to think of accused women in this novel. This goes, in Kafka's case, with his belief, shared by some existentialists, that women are more likely than men to lead an authentic existence. He implies that much when he exonerates Felice from a share of his guilt, referring to the Flaubertian phrase about living *dans le vrai* ("in the right").

How far removed from the ideas of Kierkegaard, how far removed from Pauline Christianity are Kafka's notions of the "ultimate a man can perform!" It cannot be stressed often enough, since it is constantly overlooked, what the author of *Der Prozess* repeatedly stated as his *summum bonum* ("the supreme good"): "Marrying, founding a family, accepting all the children that come, supporting them in this insecure world and even guiding them a little as well, is, I am convinced, the utmost a human being can succeed in doing at all."[39] For the aimlessly drifting big-city man and bachelor, Kafka suggested—in his fiction—the death penalty.

In order to stress K.'s weakness and helplessness, the author has created the contrast figure of the Prosecuting Attorney Hasterer, K.'s sponsor and mighty friend, superior in his profession, a "passionate eater and drinker," occupied by his women friends almost as much as by his court duties. Kafka has drawn Hasterer with sympathy. Mighty characters who were also great eaters and drinkers, like Bismarck, for example, deeply impressed him. Hasterer is a bachelor like K., and his sex life, as far as it appears in the novel, is as dubious as K.'s own; but Hasterer is, like the aforementioned Jacobsohn, a man "who sits in himself like a masterly oarsman would sit in his boat and in any boat." Even on his death bed, as will be discussed later, Kafka thought with admiration of a similarly powerful character.

K. is indeed an unlikely representative of universal man, but he is a close relative of several characters in modern literature, many of whose heroes suffer because they are "outside the Law" which is no longer easily accessible to everyone, and which can be entered only through individual gates guarded by big, ugly doubts.

Hans Castorp, for example, the quester-hero of Thomas Mann's

Magic Mountain (1924), asks himself the question about the law of his existence, but the time answers with a "hollow silence."[40] Quite modest is the guiding principle for which young Bernard in André Gide's novel *The Counterfeiters* struggles all night "with the angel." The grandiose concept "the Law" has become, in the language of Gide, *la règle* ("the rule") of which Bernard says: "...I began to ask myself how to establish a rule, since I did not accept life without a rule and yet would not accept a rule from anyone else."[41] His older friend Edouard then assures him that he must find the rule in himself. Kafka once called the Law by this modest name, which strips it of its majestic ring when he jotted down: "I have never discovered what the rule is."[42] Shortly before his horrible end K. finds out what the rule of his life should have been and states it by defining its opposite, which is his guilt: "I always wanted to snatch at the world with twenty hands, and not for a very laudable purpose, either. That was wrong, and am I to show now that not even a year's trial has taught me anything? Am I to leave this world as a man who cannot apprehend anything?"[43]

What such "laudable purposes" are is still clear to Kafka, the writer of an older generation. "Founding a family, supporting children in this insecure world, even guiding them a little," belonging to some "great soul-sustaining community," learning "a small trade." All these life goals are not even desired by Joseph K., who, at the very end of his life, realizes that his guilt was an unauthentic existence, and thus a *vie manquée*.

CHAPTER 6

"In the Penal Colony"

I By Kafka

IN October, 1914, the year he devoted, in part, to writing *Der Prozess*, Kafka wrote the story "In der Strafkolonie" ("In the Penal Colony") in two inspired vacation weeks. Through the Dreyfus affair and the early German war propaganda, the penal colonies of French Guiana and Devil's Island had become well known everywhere. Some critics quote as Kafka's inspiration Schopenhauer's suggestion "to look at this world as a place of atonement, a penitentiary so to say, a penal colony...."[1] Schopenhauer used the English expression "penal colony," at the time still an English institution (in Sydney, Australia); the French had not yet established theirs.

Even if Kafka knew this passage, this would not justify the interpreters' regarding the story as a statement of intended universal validity. Schopenhauer sees the *whole* world as a penal colony, but Kafka sees a penal colony in a world in which quite different penal systems, and cultures in which penal colonies are abhorred, exist as well.

Kafka takes pains not to have his criminal settlement identified as French, but certain similarities remain: the proximity of a great seaport and the murderous heat which in Cayenne was deservedly called *la guillotine sèche* ("the dry guillotine"). Besides, the main character in the story, the officer, speaks French with a visitor from Europe; but French is not the vernacular in that fictitious place.

The visitor is a respected, well-known European, recommended by ranking officials and invited by the commandant of the colony to witness the execution of a soldier by means of a torture machine. As the officer describes this complicated apparatus to his superior's guest, he reveals his veneration for its inventor,

108

the old commandant, and his hatred for the new one, who disapproves of the machine and the penal system which his predecessor had introduced. To win the traveler's approval and help is the main purpose behind the explanations of the officer, who, in his eagerness to acquire a helper, is unaware that, with his first words, he has inspired the foreigner's abhorrence for the apparatus. The machine, he points out, kills its victim in twelve hours of torture by stabbing deeper and deeper into the culprit's body a script of wounds spelling out the law that he has broken. This "inscription" circles the body in a narrow strip, the rest of the trunk being lacerated by baroque embellishments extending even down the arms and legs. The long needles are fastened in a glass "harrow," whose movements are directed by a "designer," into which are fed the embellished scripts.

Reverently the officer displays some of the designs, originals made by the old commandant; but the visitor cannot read them, whereas the culprit can, he is told, since he has hours to decipher them with his wounds.

Since details of Kafka's stories sometimes baffle the commentators, who then seek allegorical or psychoanalytical interpretations, it might be pointed out that the idea of inscribing something into the body of a culprit is not as fanciful as it may seem. Kafka knew such metaphors as "Dir werde ich es einbläuen, dass Du nicht lügen sollst," implying that the blue spots left by the beating will read: don't lie. And there are numerous literary examples of inscriptions on live bodies. In Ben Jonson's *Volpone,* for example, the merchant Corvino is so angered by his wife's refusal to prostitute herself in his interest that he threatens to hang her alive, bound to a dead slave, from his window, before killing her:

> "..................... inventing
> some monstrous crime, which I, in capital letters
> will eat into thy flesh with aqua fortis
> and burning corsives, on this stubborn breast."[2]

The "writing" needles of the execution machine are equipped for a similar torture, dripping a corrosive liquid into the wounds they are inflicting; but this "refinement" is now forbidden by the new commandant, as the officer angrily explains.

While the culprit is readied for execution, the traveler learns that, struck in the face with a riding whip by his officer, this man had shaken his superior and shouted: "Throw the whip away or I'll eat you raw." That the accused was not given a trial disgusts the observer even more than the torture machine did.

Kafka makes it an important point of the story that neither the officer conducting the execution nor his revered old commandant should be considered lawless tyrants or sadists. Like the inventor of the execution machine, the officer is merely practicing "sacred cruelty," his one concern in life being justice. Neither are the multitudes who witness the execution sadists. Some do not even watch at all; they lie in the sand, "eyes closed, knowing justice is being done."

The climax of the spectacle would come at the sixth hour when the most dull-witted criminal begins to decipher the inscription with his body. In former years, when the executions were still popular, the officer used to kneel down at that moment before the face of the tortured man, a small child on each arm. Now he raves: "How we all absorbed the expression of transfiguration from the tortured face. How we bathed our cheeks in the radiance of this finally achieved and quickly fading justice! What times, my comrade!"[3]

Although the execution proper has not yet begun, the visitor from the civilized world has heard and seen enough. Sensing his disapproval, the officer tries to win him over for his concept of severest justice, warning him that the new commandant with his booming voice, surrounded by silly young ladies, will see in him an ally in his struggle against the old commandant's penal system. The visitor should emphasize that he considered the old penal system as "most humane and most in consonance with human dignity."[4]

At this point, the disagreement between the new commander and the officer resembles that between Settembrini and Naphta, characters in Thomas Mann's novel *The Magic Mountain*. Settembrini, the humanist and rationalist, and Naphta, the Jesuit and believer in a communistic world state under papal guidance as envisaged by great popes of the Middle Ages, are arguing about torture and corporal as well as capital punishment: "It was not surprising that Settembrini in candid words and invoking man's dignity spoke out against this barbarous procedure in education and, above all, in the penal system." Naphta counters by defending flogging, even the *bastinado*: "According to him it was absurd to prate about human dignity, since our true dignity indwelt not in the flesh, but in the spirit.... To see something particularly disgraceful in flogging was a rather fatuous reproach."[5]

Thomas Mann himself, without agreeing with Naphta's violent views, opposed the then developing anarchy in moral values. So did Kafka; but neither he nor his fictitious observer were radicals. The visitor had come to speak out against the old system and says politely, but firmly, "no" to the demands of its strongest defender. With the ominous words: "Then it is time," the officer receives this "no" which, to him, is a death sentence and means the end of an era. Placing himself into the torture apparatus, he is killed at once by the machine, which comes apart in the process.

On the way back to the shabby houses of the colony and the palatial structure of the commandant's headquarters, the traveler, accompanied by the freed culprit and the soldier who guarded him, visits the tea house where, as he had been told by the officer, he would find the followers of the old commandant. They are there, strong but humiliated-looking dock workers, who are embarrassed when the soldier shows the stranger the grave of the old commandant, located under a table; the church had forbidden his burial in consecrated ground. On the small tombstone he reads: "Here rests the old Commandant. His adherents, who now must be nameless, have dug this grave and set up this stone. There is a prophecy that after a certain number of years the Commandant will rise again and lead his adherents from this house to recover the colony. Have faith and wait!"[6]

Thomas Mann's Naphta speaks of a similar resurrection when he says that the liberal bourgeois epoch with its ideals of humaneness is at an end, yielding to "less insipid social ideas ... which would have an admixture of sacred cruelty [*heilige Grausamkeit*], and would make it possible to see the chastisement of the carcass in a different light."[7]

In the meantime, the grotesque prophecy on the grotesquely located tombstone has been more than fulfilled. The spirit of the old commandant has been resurrected, less imposing in shape, no doubt, and starting its victory march not from a tea house in the tropics but from a beer hall in Bavaria, reestablishing penal colonies wherever he went.

The grave of the commandant has made a deep impression on the visitor, who cannot face the new commandant, whose thunderous rhetoric is impressing the cackle of geese surrounding him. Leaving the condemned man and his guard, who are chatting with friends in the tea house, he returns to the harbor. As the boat which is to take him to the ocean liner is about to take off, the freed man and the soldier race down the stairs leading to the water, to leave with him, but the traveler prevents them from jumping into the boat. The final judgment of the observer from enlightened Europe amounts to this: he does not, indeed he cannot take upon himself the responsibility of a clear decision.

The conflict between the religious and enlightened view of life and justice has reappeared in literature from time to time. The cultural change from archaic harshness to a milder, enlightened form of life and justice always entails a loss of metaphysical certainty, which is resented by a later generation. In the eighteenth and nineteenth centuries, the romantics deplored this loss and wished for the return of "the old commandant." In Germany, the most passionate lament came from Rousseau's younger German contemporary, Johann Gottfried Herder, an influential philosopher of history, literary critic, and Lutheran pastor. In one of his essays on history, Herder apostrophizes the Middle Ages: "Give us back in some respects your devotion and your superstition, your darkness and your ignorance, your disorder and crude manners, and take from us our light and disbelief, our enervated coldness and subtlety, our philosophical debility and human wretchedness."[8] Such is the value conflict of "In der Strafkolonie," the conspicuous difference being that, while Herder still lauds "the old commandant," Kafka cannot put aside the modern "light, disbelief, and enervated subtlety," feeling guilty about it, but not wishing for the return of "devotion with superstition," either. In the same evaluation of the age of enlightenment, Herder considered it unimportant "that justice was never before so humane and peace-loving."[9]

Much more violent even than Herder in praise of the old and

condemnation of the new is Stefan George, the twentieth-century German poet who was regarded by his followers as a seer. His collection of poems entitled *Der Stern des Bundes* (*The Star of the Covenant*) was one of the three preferred books German students took to the front lines of the First World War. It appeared in 1914, as did "In der Strafkolonie," whose poetic companion piece it is, and specifically so in the following poem, here rendered in prose translation:

> Those times which you call ferocious and dark
> In your own, deceitful free mild prudent one,
> They wanted through horror, torture, murder
> Through distortion, delusion, and error to reach the god.
> You felons as the first one kill the god,
> Create an idol not in his image
> Flatteringly named and gruesome as no other ever was,
> And throw your best into its maw.
> You call it YOUR way and won't rest
> Running along in arid transport until,
> You venal cowards, instead of God's red blood,
> The idol's pus flows through your veins.[10]

A violent poem; it contrasts with Kafka's work, which, although similarly violent in its imagery, is poised in its statements and thus, perhaps, more attractive than George's metric invectives. Both literary works comment on the West's long-lasting effort to substitute for metaphysically based values modern ones based on reason and goodwill, which, unfortunately, will then clash with the good will of others.

II   *By Joyce*

Literary and historical interpretations such as are given in this book will seem useless to those Kafka critics who are intent on finding allegorical presentations of the last mysteries concerning man and God in their author's work. A contributor to the critical anthology *The Kafka Problem* spoke for them all when he said: "And, of course, Kafka's problems are clarified even less by a literary-historical approach. His creative forces, rooted in that unfathomable world-anguish, lie beyond actual-

ity."[11] The confident "of course" used by so many of his colleagues
is rooted in the mistaken notion that Kafka, a saintly author,
would not stoop to anything less than universal ideas, but was
primarily interested in Christian theology.

Besides such early hagiographic criticism there are other
reasons for the many attempts to detach Kafka's works from
his real world and his worldly anguish: critics writing with
the experience of the Second World War too often ascribe their
own disgust with, or disinterest in, reality to this writer of an
older generation, to whom, on the contrary, Paris and Weimar,
lakes of Northern Italy, a small valley *der glückseligen Sonne
ausgesetzt* ("exposed to the radiant sun"),[12] a carpenter's work-
shop, rowing, swimming, horseback riding, horse races, moving
pictures, circuses, etc., were all, with varying intensity, aspects
of a reality he cherished, even if they only occasionally appear
in his works, which are predominantly metaphors and symbols
of his inner life.

Finally, there is the unfortunate coincidence that James Joyce's
Finnegans Wake, published in 1939, greatly influenced literary
critics during the forties, the decade of the "Kafka boom." The
concept of the multivalence of words and incidents in literary
works was strained by critics, and Kafka was the main victim
among German authors. A mere enumeration of some of the
spiraling meanings in *Finnegans Wake* reads like an allegorizer's
Kafka interpretation: H. C. Earwicker, the keeper of a public
house in Dublin, is Adam, Lucifer, and Humpty Dumpty, all
of whom are connected by a fall. He is the masculine principle
of creation, change and destruction, but also Tim Finnegan,
the hero of a music-hall ballad who revived during his wake, a
symbol of resurrection and renewal.

The entwined soaring motives in Joyce's work have encouraged
the majority of Kafka critics to find a profusion of grandiose
religious or existential vistas in their author. As if writing about
Finnegans Wake, the best-known Kafka translator announces
that "Kafka's most ordinary scenes have a fullness which gives
them simultaneously several meanings, one beneath the other,
until in a trivial situation we find an image of some universal
or mythical event such as the Fall. That is the way in which
his allegory works."[13] It would be better to say: that is the way

allegorizing interpreters have been working ever since the days of the Stoics whenever they encountered a widely renowned literary document whose canonic value they wanted to preserve although it offended the spirit of their age or their sensitivities. Kafka critics, inspired by Joyce, should not overlook the basic difference between these two authors: Joyce built his works with grandiose allusions which he himself names and develops, whereas they do not exist in Kafka's work but are dragged in by obviously disappointed critics.

All of Kafka's works have undergone such elevations, but none has been raised higher into religious clouds than "In der Strafkolonie." The "Rorschach method" employed by such commentators betrays itself by the vocabulary introducing the heavenly sights. Many things "suggest, make us think of, call up, may easily be related to, evoke, remind us of" something higher, the biblical God being the limit. The old Commandant, who has an authoritarian title, has constructed the torture machine, and has written in his calligraphic handwriting the precepts to be stabbed into the culprit's body—thus combining in one person "soldier, judge, engineer, chemist and draughtsman"—calls forth the commentary: "We are reminded of Jahve as He is portrayed in the Book of Exodus, fighting for the Jews against the Egyptians, setting out a code of laws, and giving detailed specifications for the construction of the tabernacle, and even for the mixing of the holy unguent."[14]

The officer, too, is allegorically promoted: "The officer, with his briefcase containing the calligraphic commandments, calls up the figure of Moses bearing the tablets of the Law, which were engraved by the Lord's own hand.... The word *Schrift* (writing) is so used as to suggest the Holy Scripture." The baroque embellishments surrounding the writing "may easily be related to the massive overgrowth of Jewish post-biblical exegesis, the confusing decorations of the Law."

A more recent critic sums up what connotations the execution of the officer evokes in the minds of the Christian allegorical school: "Interpretations have, on the whole, been confident that the story is a thinly disguised allegory of the crucifixion." Having presented the more phantastic view of another commentator, he mildly criticizes it: "The machine ... is not as likely to be an allusion to scholastic theology as to the Cross itself and its divinely ordained torture, and the idea has been put forward, not unreasonably, that the marks made by the harrow were suggested originally by the numerous small wounds covering the body of Christ in the painting by Matthias Grünewald in the Isenheim altar piece (there are also faint suggestions of a cruel sexual intercourse)."[15] They are not so faint, since everything which has holes or is pierced may have sexual implications for some critics. However, Grünewald is to be ruled out as a model since that artist was not rediscovered until the nineteen-thirties. The spread-eagle position in which the culprit is tied under the harrow reminds the theological school of the cross on which the officer, a Christ-figure, dies. But such interpreters never explain what could be Christlike about this official who is judge and executioner in one and commits suicide because his "regime" is finished.

Far from the realms of Christianity and religion in general are the literary works which "originally suggested" the "Penal Colony." There is, first of all, the novel *Le Jardin des supplices* (*The Garden of Tortures*) by Octave Mirbeau, Kafka's chief model for the basic concept and some important details of his story, as nontheological Kafka critics have discovered.[16] Mirbeau, represented by two of his works in Kafka's library, continues with *The Garden of Tortures* the tradition of the Marquis de Sade, whom he surpasses in sadistic inventiveness.

The hero of *The Garden of Tortures*, a young French scientist, is traveling in China with his English mistress, who leads him into an exotically beautiful park in which inventive executioners kill their victim, mostly paupers, for insignificant transgressions. One of these torturers, a fat man with a baby face, who looks like the executioners of Joseph K., complains while cleaning his various torture instruments after an hour's work: "Although I make an effort to save the genuine traditions, they push me aside. I am disgusted by all these new ways which the Europeans introduce under the pretext of civilization, especially the English."[17] One of the old traditions the executioner had to give up was the use of rats in his torture practice. In the same spirit, the officer complains to the traveler that the new commandant no longer allows the use of a corrosive liquid to intensify the pains of the tortured.

Just as far removed from Grünewald and biblical sources is the book which suggested the particular execution machine in Kafka's story, as he indirectly revealed: *Max und Moritz* by Wilhelm Busch. Omitted by Brod, but retained in the English translation of the Diary, are a few lines, a fragmentary sketch of another end to "The Penal Colony": "Where is the good old miller back home in the North who would stick these two grinning fellows [the culprit and his guard who are delighted with the death of the officer] beneath his millstones?"[18]

Like most German-speaking children, Kafka knew the famous "comic book" *Max und Moritz* by Wilhelm Busch, the first German "cartoonist." In this book of pictures and verses describing the evil deeds and horrible end of two evil boys, Max and Moritz, there is pictured a miraculous mill which looks like the model for Kafka's execution machine. The "good old miller" is shown standing on top of the steps to the hopper, watching with amused interest how the millstones grind the two young scamps into small pieces which a monstrous metal face spews on the floor to form there the outlines they had in life, but in spreadeagle position.

The old Commandant's machine is built like this mill: the designer resembles the hopper, the machine designs and kills at the same time, and the cogwheels which play such an important part in the story are as prominent as the cogwheel drive of the mill in Wilhelm Busch's cartoon.

The strongest argument, however, against the allegorizing school is those critics' inability to present a sustained allegorical interpretation. Only a few words, expressions, or incidents are used, and these germinal points for allegory are limited to the world of the old Commandant and the officer. There is not one elevating remark about the heavenly meaning of the new Commandant and his entourage of young ladies, nor is anything said about the important European visitor. Sometimes an overall statement is made which is as grandiose as it is obviously wrong. Kafka saw "modern existence in the symbol of an execution machine."[19] Can an existence kill and suddenly stop killing? Speaking about Kafka's attitude toward the World War, another

critic confidently calls "In der Strafkolonie" "as powerful a
commentary as that war produced."[20] The description of a gruesome torture machine used in a distant part of the world can
hardly be regarded as a commentary on the First World War.
When reading these interpretations, one seems to hear, from
time to time, the worshipful outcries of interpreters who, having
come upon a useful passage, behave like psychoanalyzing Kafka
critics who have found during their stroll through the underbrush
of Kafka's unconscious a phallic symbol here, a faintly suggested
cruel intercourse there; and the pained, infuriated outcry of
the horsewhipped soldier even leads to a fine symbol of oral
sadism.

Oral sadism, incidentally, has been mentioned as the nucleus
of "The Penal Colony." A psychoanalytical commentator writes
in the *American Imago*:

In the Penal Colony contains all the familiar symbolic action of a
nightmare and Kafka's artistic solution of his lifelong intrapsychic
conflict. The offending soldier is the instinctual self within the psyche,
the executing officer is the duplicate of the former Commandant or
primary superego, and the explorer is the conscious ego of the artist.
The torture machine is the mechanical equivalent of the devouring
mother created by the oral sadism of the culprit. The new commandant and the ladies are the symbolic representatives of mature
experience challenging the residual infantilism in the personality of
the artist-hero.[21]

But the culprit's furious outcry: "... I'll eat you raw!" is a
figure of speech used here as an outlet for great pain and fury.
Does the phrase "Well, I'll be damned" perhaps indicate hidden
religious feelings? How any critic could see maturity in the
vain, superficial new Commandant and his silly lady admirers
is as unintelligible as the identity of the infantile artist-hero.
The traveler is the outsider in the story, who has, as observer,
an important function, but he is neither the hero of the story
nor an artist.

That, of all the shorter narratives, "In der Strafkolonie" has
invited the most enthusiastic religious allegorizations seems to
be the fault of one single sentence. Explaining his penal system,
the officer remarks: "Die Schuld ist immer zweifellos." First of

all, the faulty translation: "Guilt is never to be doubted,"[22] accepted by most critics, invites generalizations about man, guilt, and punishment, not intended by Kafka whose officer says: "*The* guilt is never to be doubted" (italics mine). This statement, together with the other matter-of-fact explanations of the colony's penal system, merely implies that the guilt of an accused man is always beyond doubt, since in that little colony all cases are as simple as the present one. There exist neither hidden nor complicated crimes, nor might a crime be attributed to an innocent man.

Finally, it should be mentioned that Kafka was only mildly interested in Christian religion and its dogmas. References to Christianity in his diaries and letters are very rare; in his library of approximately 250 preserved titles, about fifty are Judaic, and two Christian, in topic, one of them a biography of Kierkegaard.

Kafka's original plan had been to have "In der Strafkolonie," together with the older stories "Das Urteil" and "Die Verwandlung," published in one book entitled *Strafen* (Punishments). The plan was dropped, and after much correspondence with his publisher Wolff, the new story appeared in 1919. In one of his letters to Kafka, Wolff remarked that the story was *peinlich* ("embarrassing"). The slightly reprimanded author answered: "To explain this last narration I only add that it is not the only thing which is embarrassing, but that, rather, our general and my particular time was and is likewise very embarrassing."[23]

CHAPTER 7

The Country Doctor Cycle

I *The Embarrassing Time*

IN calling the "general time," the time of the First World War, "embarrassing," Kafka seems to have made a frivolous understatement, and yet, apart from all its atrociousness, that time was also embarrassing to any thinking person of goodwill who had kept his reason in the general tumult. Such a person on either side of the great conflict would have to be embarrassed about the naiveté, coupled with vulgar cynicism, which appeared behind the pious affirmations of war goals made by the respective leaders. They wanted to make the world safe for democracy and their own world markets; they wanted to save the superior German virtues—and spread them geographically.

This discontent caused a desire for the great leader, the creator of the new order, the new law which might govern a pacified earth, a desire to be later abused by the Germans in an infernal fashion. At the same time, there was a feeling of resignation that, regardless of what the governments planned and did, the fate of Europe would be decided by uncontrollable forces. In 1917 the only important results of the war were beginning to appear: America entered the war, thus establishing itself as the dominant world power, Lenin returned to his homeland and, with Communism victorious, Russia's rise as a world power had begun. None of the warring parties had foreseen or wanted these results. A few years after the war, Kafka commented on the uncontrollable aspect of modern history: "The war has opened the flood gates of chaos, the buttresses of human existence are collapsing. Historical developments are no longer determined by the individual but by the masses. We are shoved, rushed, swept away."[1]

Among the "buttresses" which collapsed in Kafka's world

120

there was, above all, the "superpower" Austria-Hungary, a huge territory ruled by the House of Hapsburg, the oldest and most durable dynasty in western Europe, fated to vanish like a phantom after 1918. Kafka, the Jew in the diaspora, had thus also lost the substitute order under which he had lived, his "homeland," of which the Czechs together with the Magyars, Rumanians, and the South Slavs had been unwilling subjects.

Although still in their preparatory stage, by 1917 these developments, together with a general weariness, had created a depressing feeling of living in a time of disintegrating order. Some of the prose pieces in Kafka's Country Doctor Cycle, written during the winter of 1916–17 and the following spring, document this mood. The topical unity of most of them is the depressed feeling of the war year 1917, which appears in different historical vistas. The first, "Der Neue Advokat," is essentially a meditation about Alexander the Great. Both Kafka and Brod had seen, for years, on the classroom walls of their respective *Gymnasiums* a picture of the Pompeii mosaic: *The Battle of Alexander*. It shows how in the battle of Issus (333 B.C.) the young Macedonian hero fights his way through to the chariot of the Persian king, who is escaping capture by precipitous flight. With the customary disdain of the intellectual for the man of the sword, Brod called Alexander "a murdering so-called hero," while Kafka, also conscious of the mass slaughter connected with great historical changes, saw in Alexander the great leader in a new epoch. . In "Der neue Advokat," he contrasts the world conqueror who fought for a grandiose idea with the embarrassingly confused leaders of his own time: "Nowadays—it cannot be denied—there is no great Alexander ... no one, no one at all can lead us to India." The conquest of India, the end of the world to the ancients, had been Alexander's ultimate goal. Kafka continues: "Even in his day, the gates of India were beyond reach, yet the King's sword pointed the way to them. ... Today the gates have receded to remoter and loftier places; No one points the way; many carry swords, but only to brandish them, and the eye that tries to follow them is confused."[2]

One critic, holding the strange but not uncommon belief that "multifacetedness [*Vieldeutigkeit*] and ambiguity are the very essence of literary art,"[3] seems to consider Alexander too low in rank for a Kafka hero and elevates him to mean God. "God—in the Judaeo-Christian tradition, the association of king and God suggests itself without difficulty—provides no guidance."[4] The association king-God is very strange in this case, particularly since this king has killed his best friend, a historical fact which Kafka mentions.

The narrator of "Der neue Advokat" reports the surprising news that there is a new advocate in town, a Dr. Bucephalus, who is the reincarnation of Alexander's war-horse Bucephalus (bullhead). "There is little in his appearance to remind you that he was once Alexander of Macedonia's battle charger. . . . In general, the Bar approves the admission of Bucephalus . . . modern society being what it is . . . he deserves at least a friendly reception."[5] The commentator leaves the reader with the picture of Dr. Bucephalus peacefully studying old books by lamplight far from the hurlyburly of Alexander's great battle.

What is the function of this phantastic frame surrounding the reflections about Alexander? As is often the case with Kafka's grotesqueries, it is better to consider the feeling they evoke than to search for intellectual equations. The feeling in this case is that something great and vital is irrevocably gone from the world, a world led by bureaucrats instead of an Alexander. Finally, it should be mentioned that Kafka might well have been inspired to metamorphose the famous stallion in this grotesque way by the German invective *Bürohengst* ("office stallion").

Even more critical of Western culture is the short piece entitled "Auf der Galerie" ("Up in the Gallery"). Its first paragraph is one long, beautifully cadenced sentence describing an equestrienne repeatedly circling the ring standing on a galloping horse:

Wenn irgendeine hinfällige, lungensüchtige Kunstreiterin in der Manege auf schwankendem Pferd vor einem unermüdlichen Publikum vom peitschenschwingenden erbarmungslosen Chef monatelang ohne Unterbrechung im Kreise rundum getrieben würde, auf dem Pferde schwirrend, Küsse werfend, in der Taille sich wiegend, und wenn dieses Spiel unter dem nichtaussetzenden Brausen des Orchesters und der Ventilatoren in die immerfort weiter sich öffnende graue Zukunft sich fortsetzte, begleitet vom vergehenden und neu anschwellenden

Beifallsklatschen der Hände, die eigentlich Dampfhämmer sind—
vielleicht eilte dann ein junger Galeriebesucher die lange Treppe
durch alle Ränge hinab, stürzte in die Manege, rief das: Halt! durch
die Fanfaren des sich immer anpassenden Orchesters.

If some frail, consumptive equestrienne in the circus were to be
urged around and around on an undulating horse for months on end
without respite by a ruthless, whip-flourishing ringmaster, before an
insatiable public, whizzing along on her horse, throwing kisses,
swaying from the waist, and if this performance were likely to continue in the infinite perspective of a drab future to the unceasing
roar of the orchestra and hum of the ventilators, accompanied by
ebbing and renewed swelling bursts of applause which are really
steam hammers—then, perhaps, a young visitor to the gallery might
race down the long stairs through all the circles, rush into the ring, and
yell: Stop! against the fanfares of the ever alert orchestra.[6]

There follows a second paragraph, quite different in style:
"But since that is not so; a lovely lady, pink and white floats
in between the curtains"—and then follows a realistic description
of the same act as the audience sees it or, at any rate, is supposed
to see it. The young visitor, the only one who knows the truth
of the painful existence of the suffering performer, realizes
how futile his protest would be and weeps with frustration while
the closing march is triumphantly played.

Subtle is the way in which the "distorted" and the realistic
descriptions are fused. The distorted description of the act
is only about half as long as the realistic one. They are separated
by a short sentence which pushes the distorted part aside as if
it were an idle imagination: "But since that is not so." Significantly, the second version differs from the first not only in
style but also in its ending. In the realistic description, the
young spectator does not rush into the ring to set the world
right, but remains seated in the gallery and weeps. It becomes
clear that the distorted first part expressed what he, and he
alone, felt among unfeeling spectators. It does not seem strange,
then, that the clapping of hands was "really" a clanging of
steel-hammers.

The notion that Kafka's work is an isolated phenomenon, an
inspiration from on high, is refuted by all his works, but most
strikingly by "In the Gallery" whose motifs are all taken from

Western literary tradition: the brave outsider who saves the endangered woman, the suffering performer, for example, as represented by Goethe's Mignon and Leoncavallo's Silvio, and the circus as a symbol of Western civilization with its cotton candy goodies.

Brief as "In the Gallery" is, it is not an unimportant part of his author's "inner biography." Kafka did have aspirations like the frustrated Hamlet in the gallery. Not quite a year after he had written the story, he admitted to himself: "I can still have passing satisfaction from works like A *Country Doctor*.... But happiness only if I can raise the world into the pure, the true, and the immutable."[7]

Another narrative dealing with the embarrassing time is "Ein Bericht für eine Akademie" ("A Report to an Academy"). Its hero, a chimpanzee, not the first in the history of literature, has become a human being with the education of an average European. Asked by a learned academy to describe how he felt as an animal, the ex-ape, who has been a man for five years now, replies: "Your life as apes, gentlemen, insofar as something of that kind lies behind you, cannot be farther removed from you than mine is from me."[8] All he does remember happened after his gradual awakening to the awareness of a human being; what happened before that event others have told him.

After having been wounded and captured near the Gold Coast, he was transported on a ship in a confining cage, and his only desire was to find a way out. He found it by imitating the people around him, the good-natured but primitive sailors, whose actions and reactions were not always too different from his own. The first word he speaks, the first indication that he has crossed the borderline into a new, the human, form of being, is "hallo." From this first word to the excellent German style in which his report is written it is a long and arduous way, but the chimpanzee understood at once that his only way out of captivity was assimilation to man. The price was great, as he later realized: "Free ape, as I was, I submitted myself to that yoke."[9]

He stresses that the way out he found is not the freedom of which he speaks with such sensitivity and nobility: "I do not mean the spacious feeling of freedom in all directions. As an ape, perhaps, I knew that, and I have met men who yearned for it."[10] Here speaks, of course, Kafka himself, explaining his feelings with the same key word he had used in writing to Felice half a year before: "Having as a rule depended on others, I have an infinite longing for independence, self-reliance, freedom in all directions."[11] That ideal, of course, is unattainable, but some "way out" can be reached by the long and laborious process which leads "civilized" humans from grammar school to the desired job, degree, or profession. Anyone in our civilization, whether Westernized Jew or gentile, who has made the effort will read with smiling recognition what the ape has to say about his struggle:

"And so I learned things, gentlemen; Ah, one learns when one has to, one learns when one needs a way out; one learns at all costs. One stands over oneself with a whip. . . . With an effort which up till now has never been repeated I managed to reach the educational level of an average European. In itself that might be nothing to speak of, but it is something insofar as it has helped me out of my cage. . . ."[12]

The strong condemnation expressed in the potential subjunctive, almost as an aside, is, nevertheless a condemnation of the Western education, of which the Europeans and particularly the Germans were so proud; it could not, as history showed, ward off the one danger threatening the West which Kafka knew so well, the barbarian invasion from within. History proved him right, as well as Nietzsche, who called these educated Europeans *Bildungsphilister* ("educated philistines").

II *"A Country Doctor"*

The most phantastic of the Country Doctor stories is the title story itself. "Ein Landarzt" ("A Country Doctor") is a sequence of scenes in which realistically drawn people act in a psychologically unrealistic manner. These scenes are held together by the presence of the main character, a country doctor characterized by a resigned attitude toward life, and a quiet despair about the clashes between his medical knowledge and the superstitious customs of the villagers, as Kafka's favorite uncle, Siegfried Löwy knew it, who practiced medicine in the Moravian village of Triesch.

At the beginning of the story, the country doctor (his name is never mentioned) has been called upon to visit a seriously ill patient in a village many miles away, a stretch covered with heavy snow. The situation is hopeless since the doctor's horse has died the night before from cold and exhaustion, and Rose, the doctor's servantmaid, has tried in vain to borrow a horse in the village. Waiting in the snow and cold next to his gig, the frustrated doctor kicks the door of the old, dilapidated, and long uninhabited pigsty, which swings open. He unknowingly has started one of his deliveries, because out of the parturient pigsty crawls a stable groom, and after him wiggle, almost in prenatal position, two big horses. Kafka describes them with Homeric epithets and gives the end of the last sentence in his description the rhythm of a hexameter's second half.

... zwei Pferde, mächtige flankenstarke Tiere, schoben sich hintereinander, die Beine eng am Leib, die wohlgeformten Köpfe wie Kamele senkend, nur durch die Kraft der Wendungen ihres Rumpfes aus dem Türloch, das sie restlos ausfüllten. Aber gleich standen sie aufrecht, hochbeinig, mit dicht ausdampfendem Körper.

... two horses, enormous creatures with powerful flanks, one after the other, their legs tucked close to their bodies, each well-shaped head lowered like a camel's, by sheer strength of buttocking squeezed out through the door hole which they filled entirely. But at once they were standing up, their legs long and their bodies steaming thickly.[13]

A year later, recalling his fiction, as he sometimes did when a real-life situation resembled it, he noted, while staying in the country, "two huge horses in the stable, Homeric figures in a fleeting ray of sunshine coming through the stable window."[14] But in spite of their heroic physique, the fictitious horses are phantom horses, brother and sister of the stable groom, all three borne by the pigsty, their common mother. The groom proves his wretched ancestry immediately: when Rose walks up to him to help him harness his brother and sister, as he calls the horses, he bites her cheek viciously. With a scream she runs to the doctor for protection; he threatens the groom with a whipping but calms down because of the unexpected splendid chance for transportation. Ordering the brute to accompany him, he climbs into the gig and, still lost in admiration of the horses, does not notice the groom's disobedience. Clapping his hands and shouting: "Lively," the demon starts the horses. The doctor, having seen the girl flee into the house, extinguishing all the lights and locking the doors behind her, hears the doors being broken down by the lustful groom; but there is a rushing wind which, for a moment, befogs his senses; and suddenly the horses are stopping in front of the farm to which he was called.

The patient, a boy, whispers into his ear during the examination: "Doctor, let me die!" although there seems to be nothing wrong with him. At the thought of what is happening to poor Rose at home, the doctor is horrified, but at the same time a new feeling, a life and death wish, mingle in his mind: "I still had to see that Rose was alright, and then . . . I wanted to die too."[15] He realizes that he has sacrificed her for nothing, and with that thought, for the first time he seems to become aware of his empty bachelor's existence, his *vie manquée*. He reflects: "That I should have sacrificed Rose, . . . the pretty girl, who had lived in my house for years almost without my noticing her."[16]

His fury against the people who have destroyed his life for nothing breaks out in thoughts unuttered but which sound like complaints Kafka must have often heard made by his uncle, for example, "I was the district doctor and did my duty to the uttermost, to the point where it became almost too much. I was badly paid and yet generous and helpful to the poor. . . . The whole district made my life a torment with my night bell. . . . That is what people are like in my district. Always expecting the impossible from the doctor."[17] These complaints of a country doctor, genuine down to their cadence, form a little medical satire inserted into the deadly serious story, just as the extended legal satire contained in Huld's description of the court was inserted into *Der Prozess*. As will be shown, Kafka used this old literary device, the mixture of tragedy and comedy, again in his last novel, *The Castle*.

Preoccupied with his sorrow and regrets, the doctor approaches the bed of his patient for a second examination, and this time the boy smiles as if he "brought him perchance the most nourishing soup," which is a metaphor, meaning, like most of Kafka's food metaphors, succor for his inner life. The horses, having miraculously loosened their straps and opened the windows to observe their master, are now whinnying together, manifesting further Homeric qualities. Thus Xanthus, in the span of Achilles had warned the young hero of his approaching death. The doctor correctly interprets the whinnying as an omen: "The noise, I suppose," he says to himself, "was decreed by the powers that be to assist my examination of the patient";[18] and this time he discovers that the boy has a gaping wound in his right hip, teeming with long, thick worms. Having changed his mind, the young patient, in tears, asks to be saved, but the doctor knows that he cannot help him.

The family and the village elders approach and, with the respect due to a healer and miracle worker, undress him and put him to bed next to the boy. One Kafka critic sees here a homoerotic note in Kafka's writing, whereas another one gives a scattergun explanation: "The man is doctor, parson, lover, every guise of the god-surrogate that fails and knows itself false.... He is a doctor in the ironic sense of assuager of (sexual) pain, his own and his patient's...."[19] It seems that Kafka and the elders have something else, the miracle cure of the prophets Elijah and Elisa, in mind when these holy men lay down on the bed with two apparently dead boys, thus reviving them.

As the people undress the doctor, they sing "an extremely simple melody" to the text:

"Strip his clothes off, then he'll heal us,
If he doesn't, kill him dead!
Only a doctor, only a doctor!"[20]

This text, contradicting what is known about folksongs, cultic songs, and magic spells, appears to be an esoteric joke Kafka allowed himself with his dignified uncle Löwy (and with the reader). To imagine the kind but straitlaced gentleman stripped by superstitious villagers would certainly also amuse Kafka's father, to whom "Ein Landarzt" was dedicated, and, of course, those among Kafka's readers who knew his uncle, Dr. Löwy.

Family and elders join the teacher and the school choir outside of the house. Now, so they expect, the transfer of the miracle-worker's life strength to the boy will take place undisturbed. The dying patient, however, is indignant about the healer who cannot heal and takes up space in his deathbed. Then, recognizing his doctor's "wound," he shows an understanding which lifts him high above the dullards in his surroundings, the teacher with his silly ditty, and the simpleminded, rum-imbibing father. This very quality unfits him for his surroundings, and that is, perhaps, the meaning of his wound. He alone understands the plight of the doctor, who has no firm position in reality either. "You too were just shaken off somewhere,"[21] he says contemptuously to his strange bedfellow, then lamenting: "A fine wound is all I brought into the world; that was my sole endowment."[22] But the doctor consoles him: "Your wound is not so bad. Done in a tight corner with two strokes of the mattock. Many a one proffers his side and can hardly hear the mattock in the forest, far less that it is coming nearer to him."[23] His wound is the boy's distinction! Consoled by this idea, the boy dies. Many interpreters of the story overlook this fact, misled by the faulty translation: "Take the word of honor of an official doctor."[24] A correct translation would be: "Take the word of honor of a district-doctor with you to the beyond."

The naked doctor must save himself before the people return. Without taking the time to dress, he rolls his things into a bundle, which he throws into the gig. But now the horses move slowly through the snowy desert, and the doctor thinks about his sad fate, that he will never reach his home, which is ruined anyhow. "Naked, exposed to the frost of this most unhappy of ages, with an earthly vehicle, unearthly horses, old man, that I am, I wander astray....Betrayed! Betrayed! A false alarm on the night bell once answered—it cannot be made good, not ever."[25]

A melodious but tragic end, understandable as a metaphorical expression of gloom and rising despair which might be said to be the "meaning" of the story! Undeterred by the dreamlike, and then again whimsical, qualities of this narrative, one commentator declares: "The Country Doctor offers a prime image of humanity's dehumanization."[26] Does a little tale like "Ein

Landarzt" really speak of all mankind? Was "mankind" ever
humanized before? Kafka would not have dared to make such
apocalyptical pronouncements. Also the father-son motive has
been cited, as represented by "the fatal misunderstanding between the doctor and his patient."[27] But the boy understands
the doctor's vicarious position, and the doctor understands the
distinction bestowed upon his patient by his wound. Even
Christian allegory has been recognized in this most un-Christian
tale. "He [the boy] seems called to be a Saint or Martyr by the
wound in his side which reminds us of Christ's wound [it does
not, since it is different in shape and location]. Just as the
horses, looking in, [remind us] of Christ's birth, and the bloody
towel, which the sister of the patient waves about, of the veil
of Veronica."[28] The temptation to convert at least Kafka the
writer to Christianity seems overwhelming.

But one aspect of the story can be elucidated by interpretation
since Kafka himself has done so: the importance of the wound.
It has been noticed[29] that the doctor's first word, in describing
his patient's wound, is *rosa* ("pink"). Kafka seems to indicate
that Rose (*Rosa*) is the incurable wound of the doctor. In
August, 1917, not quite a year after he had written "Ein
Landarzt," he called Felice "his wound," interpreting his first
hemorrhage. After tuberculosis had been diagnosed in both
of his lungs he called "the wound" in his lungs "a symbol of
the wound whose inflammation is called Felice and whose depth
is called justification."[30] He wrote to Brod: "I predicted it myself. Do you remember the bloody wound in *Ein Landarzt?*"[31]

Yielding to the mood of this phantastic tale, the reader can
easily accept the demonic horses, speedy as the spirits in *Doctor
Faustus* and treacherous as such helpers are. The boy's distinction, his fatal wound, inflicted by obscure forces, is as
acceptable as the wound "Rose" which causes the doctor to
drift helplessly through the bleak winter. He is an "unhoused
man," as a German writer[32] has called the many people of our
times in whose life the protecting houses of faith, metaphysical
certainty, country, family, meaningful calling have been
destroyed.

CHAPTER 8

After the Catastrophe

I The Mind as Refuge

THAT Felice was his "wound" in more than a figurative sense, Kafka had known for a long time; but when the "wound" was diagnosed as tuberculosis in 1917, the year in which he wrote his Country Doctor stories, he was perplexed that the hoped-for solution of his personal dilemma had come in such a violent way. Brod reports his friend's melancholically waggish complaint against the deity. Kafka quoted: "I had thought he would show more finesse" (Beckmesser in Wagner's *The Mastersingers*). Tuberculosis of the lungs was, in those days, quite often a death sentence. Despite the much needed relief his illness afforded him, Kafka did not overlook its seriousness. Three months before the final break, he wrote his disconsolate fiancée a slightly veiled farewell letter, which was also a farewell to life:

And now I am going to tell you a secret which at the moment I don't even believe myself (although the distant darkness that falls about me at each attempt to work, or think, might possibly convince me), but which is bound to be true: I will never be well again. Simply because it is not the kind of tuberculosis that can be laid in a deckchair and nursed back to health, but a weapon that continues to be of supreme necessity as long as I remain alive. And both cannot remain alive.[1]

Six and a half years later, his prophecy came true. Although in the interim he went to sanatoria and summer resorts, his illness did not improve but by degrees revealed its malignity.

His first vacation stay in Zürau was, nevertheless, a comparatively happy one. He enjoyed living among the peasants in the little village and even occasionally helped with lighter

131

chores. Various studies occupied him during his half year in Zürau, particularly that of the one author whose works he had not hitherto found time to read: Kierkegaard. What Kafka says about himself and Kierkegaard does not seem to prove an often-assumed affinity between his and the Danish philosopher's views. More likely he was affected by the general enthusiasm for the incisive work of the great philosopher which had gripped the German-speaking readers—primarily students, younger intellectuals, and writers—who were rebelling against the main flaws and fallacies of their time: complacency, evolutionary optimism, chauvinism, and, above all, the naive trust that material progress would further human progress.

Even before Zürau Kafka had come in contact with Kierkegaard, reading *The Book of the Judge*, a title given to selections from the philosopher's autobiographical publications by the editor. Since autobiographies always fascinated him, it is understandable that he would choose such a work first, expecting, moreover, some similarities between its hero's unhappy engagement experience and his own; and he found them: "As I suspected, his case, despite essential differences, is very similar to mine, at least it is on the same side of the world. It bears me out like a friend."[2] The case is Kierkegaard's engagement to Regine Olsen, broken by him in obedience to strictest Christian principles as he saw them. Never in his life did the pain of this decision leave Kierkegaard, who continued to his death to think lovingly of Regine, leaving her all his belongings. Kafka repeatedly referred to him and other bachelors in the history of literature until, in 1916, angrily admonishing himself: "Give up too those nonsensical comparisons you like to make between yourself and a Flaubert, a Kierkegaard, a Grillparzer. That is simply infantile."[3]

In 1916 Kierkegaard still was to Kafka mainly the self-torturing fiancé who did not allow himself a happiness which might destroy the best in him. Not before the fall of 1917 did he begin to study the key works of the religious philosopher, whose thinking was, however, too different from his own to influence him esentially. Realizing this very soon, he wrote to the blind writer Oskar Baum, his and Max Brod's intimate friend: "Kierkegaard is a star, but above a region, almost inaccessible to me. It delights me that you are going to read him now. I only know *Fear and Trembling*."[4] A variant of this star metaphor, expressing great admiration and yet a specific rejection, occurs at the end of Kafka's Kierkegaard studies. In the spring of 1918 he informed Brod: "The roommate Kierkegaard has become a star somewhere in regard to my admiration as well as to a certain coldness in my compassion."[5]

Even in their lives, the profound difference between the two writers manifests itself: Kierkegaard attributed his becoming a writer chiefly to his sufferings because of Regina Olsen, his melancholy, and his *rixdollars* giving him the necessary leisure. Kafka's unhappy engagement lessened his creativity; not a Christian melancholia but Judaic guilt feelings about his social existence inspired him, and his lack of Austrian crowns forced him into an office which stifled it.

Just as different as their lives are the content and purpose of their writings: Kierkegaard strove to be a true Christian and, finally, to become a leader in what he considered true Christianity. Kafka was a Goethe-worshipping humanist with a Judaic anti-Goethean conscience,[6] primarily writing for himself, never thinking of preaching to his readers, and abhorring rebellion. Sharply anti-Kierkegaardian, though in the Judaic tradition, is the awe he felt before the idea of having a wife and a large family. But he expected even more than the good wife of the Proverbs could have given him. From the romantic, particularly German romantic, tradition comes his hope for secular redemption through a woman who, as his wife, would replace his *vie manquée* with fulfilled existence, or, to use his exalted vocabulary, would give him God.

In 1921, near the end of his life, Kafka's hopes had become more modest: "If I could make three wishes, I would wish, neglecting the dark desires: a recovery approximating health . . . then a foreign southern country (it must not be Palestine), and a small trade. That is not wishing much, not even wife and children are among the wishes."[7] Such satisfaction with a purely secular peaceful existence, undisturbed by feelings of sinfulness and the burning desire to find a gracious God, would have aroused Kierkegaard's contempt; a man leading such an existence he called a *pedestren* ("pedestrian"). Not even the wish

for health would have been acceptable to the Danish zealot.
When he had almost finished his last work, *The Present Moment,*
he fell ill and practically willed the end of his life at the age
of forty-two. Kafka at forty-one most unwillingly parted with
life and the young woman he loved.

Both men, masters of the poetic metaphor, might, finally, be
contrasted in their use of the metaphor of the firm steps. Kafka,
as previously quoted, wrote admiringly about Siegfried Jacobsohn's "lustiness to live, to make decisions, to set his foot joyfully
in the right place." But when Kierkegaaard sees his ideal, "the
knight of faith," in the flesh, he writes disappointedly: "How
does he walk? Firmly. He belongs wholly to the finite; and
there is no townsman dressed in his Sunday best, . . . who
treads the earth more firmly than he; he belongs altogether to
the earth, no *bourgeois* more so."[8]

At the end of his Kierkegaard studies, Kafka explained why
"the region over which that star shone" was almost inaccessible
to him: "I have not been guided into life by the hand of
Christianity—admittedly now slack and failing—as Kierkegaard
was, and have not caught the hem of the Jewish prayer shawl—
now flying away from us—as the Zionists have. I am an end
or a beginning."[9]

II *Women as Refuge*

Like the heroes of all his novels and in strictest contrast
to Kierkegaard, Kafka sought refuge with, and help from,
women. While he never set out to find female saviors, he
accepted them eagerly when given the chance. About a year
after the break with Felice he met in Schelesen, a small place
near Prague where he had gone for his cure, a young Czech
Jewess, Julie Wohryzek. He describes her as

nothing unusual, and yet amazing . . . in love with moving pictures,
operettas, powder and veils, having at her command an inexhaustible
and irrestrainable supply of the brashest Yiddish expressions, in
general quite ignorant . . . but brave in her heart, honest, unselfish . . .
such great qualities in a girl who as to physical beauty certainly
has her points, but is such a dainty littleness like the midge, flying
against the light of my lamp.[10]

He adds a few lines about her lack of understanding in intellectual matters and her disinterest in them. Nevertheless, even with this girl he had the feeling of being sheltered.

Horrified when he heard that his son wanted to marry the daughter of a shoemaker and lowly beadle in the Jewish community of a Prague suburb, old Kafka told Franz where he could go to satisfy his libido, but finally gave up his resistance. The wedding was to take place on a Sunday; two days before, the couple was informed that the apartment on which they had counted was not available, and Kafka postponed the marriage indefinitely, heeding the warnings of headaches and sleeplessness caused by the same misgivings he had felt before about marrying Felice. Even before the marriage had to be postponed, he seems to have lost interest in Julie, with whom he was never in love, as he admitted himself by talking about a "prudential match" with her. The decisive reason for the sudden termination of all relations was, however, a love affair with an extraordinary woman, Milena Jesenska-Polak. Willy Haas, the editor of Kafka's letters to Milena, compares her to a woman aristocrat of the sixteenth or seventeenth century, such as Stendhal has glorified them: "Passionate, intrepid, cool, and intelligent in her decisions, but reckless in the choice of means when her passion was involved."[11]

Milena, an only child, was raised, after her mother's early death, by her tyrannical father, Dr. Jan Jesensky, scion of an old respected Prague family and oral surgeon at the University of Prague. She reacted with a lifelong burning desire for freedom and hatred for all injustice. Being sent to *Minerva*, the first Czech *Gymnasium* for girls, she acquired an excellent education and became the leader of young *Minervists* rebelling against the stuffiness and hypocrisy prevailing in "the good families" from which they all came. They were too individualistic to belong to the contemporary European youth movement; their goals were those of the feminist movement of the day whose most important forerunner in Bohemia had been Božena Němcová, author of the story *Babička* ("Grandmother"), an important inspiration for Kafka's novel *Das Schloss* (*The Castle*). Dr. Jesensky, severe and conservative, despised his daughter's unbreakable will to live intellectually, emotionally, and sensuously

with all the intensity her great vitality was capable of. Unfortunately for her, she entered into a liaison with Ernst Polak,
a Jewish intellectual, admired by his circle of writer friends
because of his sharp mind and critical taste in literary matters,
but an amoral cynic and egotist. Like other men of his type, he
greatly attracted women, and Milena, who suffered from his
cruelty toward her, could not break away from him until four
years after she had met Kafka. Her anti-Semitic father was
powerless although not inactive. To separate her from Polak,
at that time still her lover, he sent her to a mental hospital,
where she had to stay for nine months—only to marry Polak
as soon as she was dismissed and to live with him in Vienna,
far away from her father.

Without any support from her husband and her father, she
had to work hard not to starve in the difficult years after the
First World War. Carrying baggage in the Vienna railroad
station, teaching Czech to Germans, among them Hermann
Broch, she survived until at last she discovered her talent as a
writer and became a well-known journalist. In the course of
her literary life, she published three books of feuilletons, her
favorite literary form, and, as a result of having to cook for
boarders later in her life, even a cookbook. As regular contributor to respected Prague papers and columnist for one of
them, she had risen as high as she could in her profession.
About her talent she remarked in her unmistakable style: "The
only thing I can write are love letters, and, really, my articles
are just that."[12]

Milena had known Kafka when she was a member of Prague's
literary and artistic circles, but not before 1920 had she read
any of his publications. Deeply impressed, she asked and, surprisingly enough, received, his permission to translate into
Czech "Der Heizer," the first chapter of the novel Amerika. Even
the fact that she wanted to publish it in the Communist magazine
Kmen did not deter him. He could foresee as little as his
translator that, with this publication, he would become for
many Communist critics a fighter in the class war. Milena's
choice of Stanislav Neumann, a Communist writer and the
editor of Kmen, was not political. Since she had not yet acquired
a name as a columnist, she was happy to know that a respected

publisher like Neumann, whom she happened to know, surrendered an entire number of his weekly *Kmen* to her labor of love. In his editorial remarks, Neumann only praised the literary excellence of "Der Heizer," but in his necrologue on Kafka he saw in it a socialist story about a suffering worker before the haughty men of power and wealth. Consequently he eulogized the dead author as a mind-mate: "He [Kafka] was a sensitive spirit who looked deeply into the organism of today's unjust society; he loved the oppressed and mercilessly flogged the rich in a very complicated, but moving way."[13] No such complicated flogging takes place in the first chapter of *Amerika.* The conflict between discipline and justice which it describes is usually solved in favor of discipline on ships as well as in armies and radical parties.

The necessary correspondence between the author of "Der Heizer," who was in Merano, and Milena in Vienna soon led to an epistolary love affair and, as before, Kafka began to crave the narcotic of love letters, avoiding a meeting with their writer as long as possible. Using a metaphor more harmless than "narcotic," he describes this craving in a letter to her:

What's your guess? Can I still get a letter by Sunday? It should be possible. But it's crazy, this passion for letters. Isn't a single one sufficient? Isn't knowing once sufficient? Certainly, it's sufficient, but nevertheless one leans back and drinks in the letters and is aware of nothing but that one doesn't want to stop drinking. Explain this, Milena, teacher![14]

Soon he begins to warn her, by speaking of the "journey of the thirty-eight years" which lies behind him. A metaphorical description of their contrasting style of life shows early that this relation could not last: "You're standing firmly near a tree, young, beautiful, your eyes subduing with their radiance the suffering world . . . I'm creeping in the shade from one tree to another. . . . You're trying to give me courage, are aghast at my faltering steps [again the metaphor of the uncertain steps] . . . I can't do it, I fall down. . . ."[15]

Milena, however, wanted her lover, and she stormed at the tired man in Merano until, on his way back to Prague, he stopped for four days to be with her in Vienna. The four days they met as lovers gave Kafka a passing happiness, but a shorter meeting a few weeks later in the bordertown of Gmünd, consisting only of laments and discussions, resembled the unhappy meeting with Felice in the border station Bodenbach.

Late in the fall of 1920, the year in which their love began, Kafka writes: "I'd be terribly mistaken if the idea that we now cease writing to one another didn't turn out to be a good one. But I'm not mistaken, Milena.... They [the letters] can't do anything but produce a day in Gmünd, produce misunderstandings, humiliation, almost perpetual humiliation."[16] He also begged her not to try to see him again. Milena was confronted with the same gentle but irrevocable rejection which Julie had faced a few months earlier. Neither Kafka nor Milena ended their relation abruptly. At long intervals, they wrote each other until 1923, and Milena visited him a few times in Prague. Kafka called these visits "sick-bed calls." In a melancholy epilogue to the whole affair he wrote in one of his last letters: "I must confess that I once envied someone very much because he was loved, in good care, guarded by reason and strength, and lay peacefully under flowers."[17] Those flowers grew in the vicinity of Vienna, where Milena and Kafka hiked during their four-day tryst. The melancholy lover sought refuge from ills of his world with a woman twelve years his junior whom, significantly enough, he sometimes called "mother Milena." Once he even addressed his youngest sister Ottla, who did much to shelter him, as "great mother."

In his Kafka biography, Max Brod published the letters of despair in which Milena sought his advice. Kafka, however, asked Brod to help him prevent a meeting with Milena. In the same letter, he continues: "But if you fulfill my wish, you must not at the same time repeat that you do not understand me." And now he informs Brod, not by hints, as before, but "speaking bluntly," why this must be. He speaks of "a sickening of the instinct, a result of our time." He confesses that every second girl appeals to him physically, except Felice and Milena. He ends this intimate confession with the surprising remark: "Obviously because of my dignity, my arrogance (no matter how humble he looks, the crummy westernized Jew) I can love only that which is so high above me that it is out of my reach."[18]

The remark is as exaggerated as most of the derogatory statements Kafka made about himself and as unconsciously insincere as his groveling in the dust before Milena in the early stage of their affair.

Even though he could not love her, Kafka realized that Milena understood him better than anyone else. He proved his deep trust in her by giving her some of his manuscripts and, most importantly, his diaries without ever asking for their return. After his death she sent them to Brod, who published them.

Milena's moving letters to Brod about her frustrated love and her deep sorrow after Kafka's death contain passages like the following, surpassing anything other contemporaries had to say about him:

> But Frank cannot live. Frank does not have the capacity for living. Frank will never get well. Frank will die soon. For, obviously, we are capable of living because at some time or other we took refuge in lies, in blindness, in enthusiasm, in optimism, in some conviction or other, in pessimism or something of that sort. But he has never escaped to any such sheltering refuge, none at all. He is absolutely incapable of *lying*, just as he is incapable of getting drunk. He possesses not the slightest refuge.[19]

Later in life she saw her love affair with Kafka differently: "I was probably fated," she told her biographer Margarete Buber-Neumann, "to love only weak men. None really ever looked out for me and none sheltered me. A woman is punished when she has too much initiative."[20] This conversation took place in a Nazi concentration camp where Milena languished four years for having helped Jews and other "undesirables" to flee. Undernourishment and general neglect killed her in 1944.

CHAPTER 9

The Castle

I Approach to the Castle

WHILE Kafka was in Prague in 1921 he was sheltered by the police. In the years after the war, anti-Semitism had become stronger again, and he informs Milena of one such outbreak in his hometown:

I've spent all afternoon in the streets, wallowing in the Jew-baiting. "Prašivé plemeno"—"filthy rabble" I heard someone call the Jews the other day. Isn't it the natural thing to leave the place where one is hated so much? . . . The heroism which consists of staying on in spite of it all is that of cockroaches which also can't be exterminated from the bathroom.—Just now I looked out of the window: Mounted police, *gendarmerie* ready for the bayonet charge, a screaming crowd dispersing, and up here in the window the loathsome disgrace of living all the time under protection.[1]

Milena's anti-Semitic father, Kafka believed, would not be able to see the difference between her husband and her friend—"for the European we both have the same Negro face."[2]

Encountering, at the same time, the revived anti-Semitism of the streets and the salons deepened his feeling that he did not belong and renewed his desire to leave. After he had started work on *Das Schloss* (*The Castle*), his last novel, he wrote "Der Aufbruch" ("The Departure"), a prose piece of fourteen lines which repeats, in a different setting, a motif of the novel: The master has mounted his horse to start out on a journey. Asked by his servant at the city gate where he is riding, he answers: "I do not know, just out of here, just out of here. Out of here, nothing else, it's the only way I can reach my goal." When the servant replies: "So you know your goal?" the master says: "Yes, I've just told you. Out of here, that's my goal."[3]

140

In the early twenties, before work on *Das Schloss* was begun, Kafka's diaries and letters again contain certain metaphors and phrases anticipating the creative act, being related, as they are, to the dominant feelings, moods, actions, thoughts, and incidents of the still unwritten work. The first and most informative such harbinger of *Das Schloss* is a passage in a letter to Milena dating from 1920. The writer identifies himself with a filthy beast in the woods who has seen "the most wonderful sight" he ever came upon—Milena. "... I came closer—though fearful in this new freedom which was, nevertheless, *the freedom of the homeland*—came closer nevertheless, ... laid my face in your hand, I was so happy, so proud, so free, so powerful, *so at home—over and over again this: So at home*" (italics mine). Kafka had been the opposite before: unhappy, humiliated, unfree, weak, and, worst of all, homeless. All through the novel, as far as it was written, these are the basic sorrows of the hero K., who does not even find the temporary relief of his creator. But this happiness could not last. The same letter continues: "It grew more and more clear to me what an unclean vexation, what an obstacle I was for you, hindering you everywhere, ... I remembered who I am, no longer saw any deception in your eyes, I experienced the dream fright (of *behaving as though one were at home in a place where one does not belong*)."[4] It is this nightmarish situation in which K. lives in the novel.

Phantasies of leaving the place of oppression, of finding "Canaan," occupied Kafka in 1921 and early 1922. There is the previously quoted passage, in a 1921 letter, about his three wishes, one of them being life in "a foreign southern country (it must not be Palestine)." Diary entries of the same time, and later ones, deal with the exodus motif brought all the more to Kafka's mind as he approached his fortieth year, the number forty reminding him of the forty years Israel wandered through the desert according to *Exodus*. Three months before he started *Das Schloss*, this motif begins to appear in his diary: "The essence of the Wandering in the Wilderness. A man who takes this journey as the national leader of his organism with a shred (more is unthinkable) of consciousness of what is happening. He is on the track of Canaan all his life. ..."[5]

In spite of the feeble remnants of Judaism in his father's world, Kafka contrasts this world with the non-Jewish West:

... Why did I want to quit the world [of the father]? Because "he" [the father] would not let me live in it, in his world. Though indeed I should not judge the matter so precisely, for I am now a citizen of this other world [the Western world], whose relationship to the ordinary one [the world of the father] is the relationship of the wilderness to cultivated land (I have been forty years wandering from Canaan); I look back at it like a foreigner, though in this other world as well—it is the paternal heritage I carry with me—I am the most insignificant and timid of all creatures and am able to keep alive thanks only to the special nature of its arrangements; in this world it is possible even for the humblest to be raised to the heights as if with lightning speed, though they can also be crushed by thousand-year old forces exerting the pressure of an ocean [the thousand years, stated with poetic license,[6] represent the time span during which Jews have been persecuted in the Christian world]. Should I not be thankful despite everything? Was it certain that I should find my way to this world? Could not "banishment" from one side, coming together with rejection from this, have crushed me at the border? ... It is indeed a kind of Wandering in the Wilderness in reverse that I am undergoing: I think that I am continuously skirting the wilderness and am full of childish hopes (particularly as regards women) that "perhaps I shall keep in Canaan after all"—when all the while I have been decades in the wilderness and these hopes are merely mirages born of despair, especially at these times when I am the wretchedest of creatures in the desert too, and Canaan is perforce my only Promised Land, for no third land exists for mankind.[7]

In the metaphoric use of "wilderness" and "Canaan," the concept "land" signifies a way of life and also a state of the soul. Kafka uses wilderness as a metaphor for the civilization of the West, whose worth had become more doubtful than ever. One of the many indications revealing the mood of the time is the popularity enjoyed by Oswald Spengler's The Decline of the West; another is T. S. Eliot's poem The Waste Land, published in 1922, the year in which Kafka wrote Das Schloss, which is located in the waste land.

The diary entry of January 28 was continued the next day

with a comment on his stay in Spindlermühle (Spindelmühle), a winter resort in the Riesengebirge:

> My situation in this world would seem to be a dreadful one, alone here in Spindelmühle, on a forsaken road, moreover, where one keeps slipping in the snow in the dark, a senseless road, moreover, without an earthly goal (to the bridge? Why there? Besides, I didn't even go that far); I too forsaken in this place (I cannot place a human, personal value on the help the doctor gives me, I haven't earned it; at bottom the fee is my only relationship to him), incapable of striking up a friendship with anyone, incapable of tolerating a friendship . . . I am too far away, am banished.[8]

Soon afterward, the snow-covered road and the bridge reappeared in the opening paragraphs of *Das Schloss*. As the hero K. stands on the bridge "which led from the road to the village," he looks up into the apparent emptiness where the Castle, shrouded by fog and darkness, is completely hidden from view. Snow, darkness, solitude—the mood of the novel is created and a first impression of the Castle's evasiveness conveyed.

In the village inn, K. introduces himself, pretending ignorance of where he is and finally maintaining that the Lord of the Castle, Count Westwest, has hired him as land surveyor, his assistants being scheduled to arrive the next day by coach. Both are lies, as a telephone call from the inn to an under-castellan reveals; but before the wrath of those present against this "common, lying vagabond and probably something worse" can break loose the telephone rings again and a higher official announces that a K. was indeed appointed as surveyor. This is not the rectification of a previous error, but, as K. understands at once, it shows that the Castle is informed about him. Pretending that his claim is genuine, smilingly he accepts the battle. Nowhere does the novel indicate how the Castle knows about K. and what or where he was before he set out on this uncertain and long journey.

The initial situation is weird, and the further developments of the novel are a Kafkaesque blending of realism and events and attitudes which are humanly possible but will never occur, like the beginning contest between a Castle full of officials and

a lonely bachelor in his thirties, who is, according to all that
is revealed, an intruder.

On the next morning, K. takes a walk to become familiar with
the Castle now clearly visible on its hill, with only one tower
above the manor house, which is circled by flocks of crows. In
one of his aphorisms, Kafka says: "The crows maintain that a
single crow could destroy the heavens. There is no doubt of
that, but it proves nothing against the heavens, for heaven
simply means: the impossibility of crows."⁹ The crows alone,
according to the Western literary tradition, indicate the negative,
even ominous character of the Castle as further elaborated in
the following sentences: It is not an imposing building, but a
complex of crumbling houses "hardly superior" to those in
K.'s native town.

If it was merely a question of enjoying the view . . . K. would have
done better to revisit his native town, which he had not seen for
such a long time. And in his mind he compared the church tower
at home with the tower above him. The church tower, . . . an earthly
building—what else can man build?—but with a loftier goal than
the humble dwelling houses (they constitute the main part of the
Castle), and a clearer meaning than the muddle of everyday life.
The tower above him here . . . the tower of a house, as was now
evident, was uniformly round, part of it graciously mantled with
ivy, pierced by small windows that glittered in the sun—with a
somewhat maniacal glitter and topped by what looked like an attic,
with battlements that were irregular, broken, fumbling, as if designed
by the trembling or careless hand of a child, clearly outlined against
the blue. It was as if a melancholy-mad tenant who ought to have
been kept locked in the topmost chamber of the house had burst
through the roof and lifted himself up to the gaze of the world.¹⁰

It should be noted here that the English translation renders
gnädig vom Efeu bedeckt ("mercifully hidden by ivy") as
"graciously mantled with ivy" thus weakening the strikingly
derogatory remarks about the Castle and making it more in-
habitable for the divine powers and abstractions which dwell
there according to many critics.

Aside from the Castle, there are two other buildings which
attract K.'s attention: the village church and the school. Kafka's

terse style does not provide the reader with resting points. The author does not pause to create a picturesque background and certainly does not allow himself any *chevilles* ("stopgaps"). K.'s impressions of these buildings at the very beginning of the novel demand closer attention than would merely descriptive passages. Having stopped at the village church, he notices that "it was really only a chapel, widened with barnlike additions so as to accommodate the parishioners." This village church has developed its peripheral functions, but not undergone organic change, just as did the Western churches which were unable to cope inwardly with the new age. The school, right behind the church, shows the same significant defect, strangely combining "a look of great age with a provisional appearance."[11] An admirably concise statement not only of Western education's dilemma, but also of the dilemma of Western culture; how to preserve very old traditions the faith in which is dwindling, and how to cope with new problems, met so far by improvisations, not solutions.

The fact that a count is almost absolute ruler over a small territory, together with the general use of the telephone, establish the locale and the time of the novel in Central Europe during the last decades before the First World War. The three buildings introduce the reader to a land where senility and insanity prevail, and around whose highest point the birds of death are circling—a waste land. It is the territory of the Count with the suggestive name Westwest, familiar to Kafka, who called himself "the most Westernized Jew," being as little proud of that achievement as his humanized chimpanzee was of the European education he had acquired with so much labor.

The West was not Canaan. Kafka caught only fleeting glances of that land of the soul when, for example, he watched enviously a little East Jewish boy playing in the hall where a group of Galician Jews were staying overnight on their way to the United States.[12] The official Dr. jur. Kafka knew that he could not settle among Galician Jews, that he could just as little return to the churchtower of a simpler, but authentic society, as he could be a little boy again. He knew he had to struggle on like K. to be accepted in Count Westwest's hostile territory. The symbolism of the buildings makes it clear that such struggles are in store for all sensitive outsiders, not only Westernized Jews—all of them being suspect to the vast majority of the West satisfied with spurious values and taboos blindly obeyed. The villagers of Count Westwest's domain consider these outsiders dangerous, at best intruders, who have entered their land under pretense; at worst, they are considered alien vagabonds who should be expelled. But these K.'s who wander over the snow-covered road of exile try again and again to find a "position" in the senile and insane world of the Count, since there is "no third land" in which they can settle. K. also is not Everyman, and his problems are not religious, even though he strives with religious fervor for a meaningful life. It is a difficult goal for an outsider to achieve, and requires, in the Western world, struggles with bureaucracies and suspicious fellow citizens. What makes K., above all, an outsider are his reminiscences of an authentic existence and the "religious" seriousness with which he strives to achieve that state again.

II *The Siege*

Count Westwest's subjects are as questionable by "normal" standards as his dominion's representative buildings. There is the timid landlord, overawed by the Castle as well as his "door-filling" spouse. There is, still well known to any old Central European, the subaltern official, yelling insults at his victims, and the teacher, "a dictatorial little man," wielding the feared cane, threatening to "crush" anyone who disobeys him, all of them accepting taboos even stranger than those their contemporaries obeyed in reality. When K. asks the teacher whether he knows the Count, the shocked pedagogue answers: "How could I?" and adds in French: "Please remember that there are innocent children present." In this world of devoted subjects (*Untertanen*), the mentioning of his exalted highness is a taboo.[13]

The same lack of understanding and kindness and the same strict obedience to odd taboos characterize the peasant population of the village. Marching through the deep snow without ever getting closer to the Castle, K. finally knocks at the door of one of the peasants. Admitted by a confused old man, he finds himself in a huge kitchen where a woman is washing clothes, children are playing, and two men are taking a bath in a huge wooden tub. This idyllic Brueghelian scene, however, is deceptive. After K., collapsed on a chest, has fallen asleep, he is awakened by the bathers, now dressed, and is informed: "Land-surveyor, you can't stay here. Excuse the discourtesy . . . , but hospitality is not our custom here. . . . We small people stick to our tradition, you can't blame us for that."[14] K. understands and asks a refined-looking young woman whom he had not noticed when he entered, who she is. She has just time to say: "A girl from the Castle," when the two men almost carry him out and deposit him in front of the door. More to remove him from the vicinity than to help him, the old drayman Gerstäcker brings out a horse-drawn sledge and takes the completely exhausted K. back to the inn.

As the castle which K. wanted to visit on that day recedes again, "a bell began to ring merrily up there that for at least a second made his heart palpitate, for its tone was menacing too, as if it threatened him with the fulfillment of his vague desire."[15] Passages like these, having a religious ring, occur occasionally in the novel, but they are not religious in the Christian or even Kierkegaardian sense in which so many interpreters understand them. To K. as well as to Kafka, belonging, working at a meaningful task, and being a respected man in a national community among one's peers were ultimate and therefore religious goals.

As so often in Kafka's novels, the ridiculous follows immediately upon the sublime. Walking up the steps leading to the Inn by the Bridge, K. is met by two assistants whom the Castle has sent him, although it does not employ him. It is part of a cruel game the officials are playing with him since these assistants, two boyish-looking young men, will plague K. with their disobedience and continuous clowning. For the moment, however, K. laughs with pleasure when they receive him with a military salute, reminding him of his service in the army, "those happy times." K.'s reaction to the salute reveals much about his inner life. He lives at an age of Western civilization in which any sensitive European was conscious of the complete lack of purpose and sensible leadership, the "hollow silence" life opposed, according to Thomas Mann, to all questions as to

the meaning of a young man's efforts and aspirations. Many a
returned soldier in the Europe of Kafka's time looked back, as
did K., with pleasure to the time of his military service; when
he knew exactly what to do and did not have to yield to fruitless
reflections, when the inner self was on vacation, no matter how
hard the outer one had to work.

As their first duty, the assistants have to telephone the Castle
and inquire whether K. may pay it a visit. The answer, which
is definitive as the subsequent events of the novel show, is:
"No—neither tomorrow nor at any other time." Now K. himself
goes to the telephone and hears what he had never heard before,
the humming sound of "countless children's voices—but yet not
a hum, the echo rather of voices singing at an infinite distance—
blended by sheer impossibility into one high but resonant sound
that vibrated on the ear as if it were trying to penetrate beyond
mere hearing."[16] Again we note the religious undertone. This
time it is similar to the ringing of the Castle bell, the musical
echo of K.'s deepest longing; but like anything which comes
from the Castle, it is meaningless for him, or sheer mockery.
The mysterious singing, he later learns from the Mayor, sounds
to the people in the village like singing, but the sound is caused
by the official's continuous use of the phone. "This humming
and singing . . . is the only real and reliable thing you'll hear;
everything else is deceptive." The telephone connection between
the village and the Castle is turned off, and only now and then
"a fatigued official may feel the need for a little distraction"[17]
and connects himself with the village. The answer they receive
then is nothing but a joke. That the central European officials
liked to joke sadistically with inferior clients is, incidentally, a
historical fact.

A similar joke is the letter K. receives from the Castle right
after his arrival, telling him that he is now in the Count's
service and that everything possible will be done to keep him
contented with his work. This letter is delivered by a young
man called Barnabas who initially seems to K. almost like a
heavenly apparition since he thinks he will take him to the
Castle. But he also knows that the entry to the Castle can only
be granted by the man who sent the letter, his ultimate superior,
the head of Division X, the powerful official Klamm.

Believing that Barnabas will return to Klamm in the castle, K. accompanies him; but Barnabas takes him to his home, where he lives with his two sisters Olga and Amalia and his invalid parents. K. feels somehow the "curse" which lies on this family, and when Olga goes to the *Herrenhof*, the inn where the officials stay during their sojourn in the village, K. accompanies her. Now the topsy-turvy character of this small world is, for the first time, fully revealed: The innkeeper of the *Herrenhof* cannot grant K.'s request to stay there overnight, not even in some corner, "because the gentlemen (the officials) are so sensitive that I'm convinced they couldn't bear the sight of a stranger, at least unless they were prepared for it; and if I were to let you sleep here and by some chance ... you were discovered, not only would it mean my ruin, but yours too. That sounds ridiculous, but it's true."[18]

This is not the only ridiculous aspect of this strange world. In the barroom, K. meets the barmaid Frieda who does him the unexpected favor of letting him see Klamm—of course only from a distance, through a peephole in the door. In the light of a dangling light bulb above his desk K. sees mighty Klamm, a fat, ponderous gentleman of medium height. Although he has a Virginia cigar in his hand, he sleeps. It is his "sleeping position," Frieda informs him. "The gentlemen do sleep a great deal, it's hard to understand."[19]

Strange like everything in this world is the sudden love of Frieda and K., consummated behind the bar on the floor between puddles of beer. During their lovemaking, Klamm calls Frieda from the adjoining room, but she disobeys and calls out defiantly that she is with the land-surveyor. Until then, she had been Klamm's mistress, a most honorable position in this world ruled by officials. Everyone speaks with respect of her closeness to the mighty one who, for many years, has been selecting bed companions from the feminine population of the Count's village.

One of the other maidens deigned worthy of the honor was, "much more than twenty years ago," the Bridge Inn's landlady. From her enraptured yet melancholy report, the outsider K. learns that Klamm never talks to his "loves," never gives presents, but allows them to take something that happens to lie around as a souvenir. So the landlady still cherishes a photograph, almost

unrecognizable because of age and much use. After careful
examination K. makes out that it shows a young man clearing
the rope in a high jump. It is, so the landlady informs him, the
messenger who ordered her to come to Klamm. These messengers
of the officials have to practice high jumping to stay agile. Three
times she was ordered to Klamm's bed, and no more. Why it
all ended so soon the still grieving landlady cannot understand,
although during the first years of her marriage to timid Hans
she and her husband discussed this problem in lengthy pillow
conversations. She knows how bizarre this must sound to the
outsider K.:

"If I try very hard I can of course think myself into your ideas,
valid, perhaps, in the very different land you come from. But it's
next thing to madness to imagine that Klamm could have given me
Hans as a husband simply that I might have no great difficulty in
going to him if he should summon me some time again. Where is
the man who could hinder me from running to Klamm if Klamm
lifted his little finger? Madness, absolute madness; one begins to feel
confused oneself when one plays with such mad ideas."[20]

In Frieda's longer affair with Klamm, the landlady has relived
the great experience of her life and now is K.'s enemy because
he has taken Frieda away from Klamm. She cannot understand
why her beloved little one has left the "eagle" to join the
"gartersnake." This heroic comparison strikes K. as ridiculous,
but a few days later he accepts it:

He [K.] thought of Klamm's remoteness, of his impregnable dwelling, of his silence, broken perhaps only by cries such as K. had
never yet heard, of his downward-pressing gaze, which could never
be proved or disproved, of his wheelings, which could never be
disturbed by anything that K. did down below, which far above he
followed at the behest of incomprehensible laws and which only for
instants were visible—all these things Klamm and the eagle had in
common.[21]

Kafka obviously enjoyed his character Klamm. In a deleted
passage, K. thinks of forcing Klamm to listen to him, and the
landlady reacts with contempt: "Compel him to hear you! . . .
Compel the lion to eat straw! What deeds of heroism!"[22] All

through the novel Kafka ridicules the fat village pasha, but the critics are not amused, they are edified by him. Kafka, always conscious of the names he gave his characters, called this official Klamm, and *klamm* suggests to the German reader a row of disagreeable qualities: tight, narrow, scarce, numb, clammy, damp. And yet, the obese, indolent lecher is supposed to be, according to many critics, a member of the heavenly hierarchy.

A visit with the Mayor of the village makes K. realize how difficult his battle will be. He hears at once the complete disagreeable truth that the village does not need a land-surveyor. The Mayor explains how, many years ago, some department in the Castle decreed that a land-surveyor should be employed; but he had answered that the village did not consider such an appointment necessary, although some villagers disagreed. The confusion caused by administrative mistake has not been solved until now. Nowhere in the novel does it say how K. came to know about the possible need for a land-surveyor. That he was never employed or even invited by the Castle is certain. But the possible need for such a man in the future is alive enough in some departments, so that their officials accept K.'s intrusion in order to play a cruel game with him. Trying to help K., the Mayor has his wife search through a mountain of documents for the paper concerning the employment of a land-surveyor. What worries the Mayor more than the missing document are the pedantic investigations of the secretary Sordini who, unfortunately for the Mayor, knows about the case. K. is told how the walls in the office of this eminently industrious official are covered with huge columns consisting of documents piled on top of each other. Since files are constantly taken from and added to these bundles, the columns continuously collapse, and the crashing sounds repeated at short intervals, have become typical of Sordini's office. K. reacts bitterly to these revelations:

"Mr. Mayor, you always call my case one of the smallest, and yet it has given hosts of officials a great deal of trouble, and if, perhaps, it was unimportant at the start, yet through the diligence of officials of Sordini's type it has grown into a great affair. Very much against my will, unfortunately, for my ambition doesn't run to seeing columns of documents, all about me, rising and crashing down, but to working quietly at my drawing-board as a humble land-surveyor."[23]

Meaningful work, and his uncontested right to exist unmolested by official and unofficial hostilities, were Kafka's and K.'s goals.

After the Mayor has given him an insight into the complicated bureaucracy of the Castle and shows his annoyance that K. finds his description entertaining, K. comments: "It only amuses me, because it gives me an insight into the ludicrous bungling that in certain circumstances may decide the life of a human being."[24] The reasons that make him stay so tenaciously in the inhospitable village are enumerated by him: "The sacrifice I made in leaving my home, the long and difficult journey, the well-grounded hopes I built on my engagement here, my complete lack of means, the impossibility after this of finding some other suitable job at home, and last but not least my fiancée, who lives here."[25]

What justifies his hopes of finding employment in the Count's realm is never mentioned in the novel, but it seems that Kafka planned to give that explanation in a part never actually written. One such explanation of opaque events appears, however, later in the novel. After K. has dismissed the assistants, one of them explains that they were sent to him by Galater, the official deputizing for Klamm at K.'s arrival in the village. They informed Galater that they did not know anything about surveying, but were told by him: "That's not the main point; if it's necessary, he'll teach it to you. The main thing is to cheer him up a little. According to the reports I've received he takes everything too seriously. He has just got to the village and starts off thinking that a great experience, whereas in reality it's nothing at all. You must make him see that."[26]

Galater himself has shown that he takes trifles very seriously where his own well-being is concerned. When, a few years before the arrival of K., dry wood stored too near a hot stove in his office began to smoke, he alarmed the fire department and, although the wood did not smoke any longer, insisted on being carried out by a fireman since he was too fat to move quickly. Whenever Kafka speaks of the officials, he shows them to be malicious or ridiculous. It was probably also Galater who wrote the two confusing letters which Klamm signed, for it is unlikely that the lazy Klamm had composed them. From what Galater had said to the assistants, the reader must assume that the possibility for K. to be used as land-surveyor actually existed. On returning from his interview with the Mayor, K. is told by the landlady to leave her inn immediately. She cannot forgive him his lack of respect for the high official whose mistress he has taken away and is planning to marry. Fortunately for K., the Mayor, being only partly an official, understands his plight and finds him a temporary position as school janitor. K. and Frieda must live in one of the two classrooms whenever it is not occupied. Their relationship, the teacher tells him, must be legalized as fast as possible, as underlings are not being allowed to live the free life of officials.

Before K. goes to his schoolroom, he waits for two hours in the courtyard of the *Herrenhof* next to and inside Klamm's sleigh in order to speak to him when he leaves. Foxy Klamm, however, has seen him, and does not leave until his secretary has led K. away. Fatigued by his long wait, K. oversleeps the next morning, causing a disturbance; and when the teacher finds out that he also had broken into the woodshed during the night, he dismisses him.

III   *The Siege is Ended*

The dismissal of K. after his short career as a school janitor marks the turning point of the novel as far as Kafka has written it. Everything developed since his arrival in the village now comes to a sudden end: he, the dismissed janitor, dismisses his assistants, and Frieda breaks with him. The reason for their dismissal was their continuous clowning and their flirting with Frieda, who encouraged them. Locking the door behind the two surprised young men, K. leaves them out in the cold winter morning, implacable in spite of their whining and knocking at the window panes. In a fearful discussion with her fiancé, Frieda expresses her justified suspicion that she was primarily a means for gaining access to Klamm. After K. leaves for the Barnabas home to see whether there is a message for him, she allows herself to be pulled through the broken window by Jeremias, one of the assistants, with whom she returns to the *Herrenhof* to work again as a barmaid; Jeremias becomes a room waiter and lives, for the time being, with Frieda in her room.

K.'s visit with Olga leads to her long "confession" of why

she and her family have to live as outcasts. Before the misfortune, her father had been the best shoemaker in the village
and the third training supervisor of the fire department. During
a village festival occasioned by the Castle's gift of a new fire
engine, the official Sortini, a "small, weak, pensive gentleman"
jumped with "his legs stiff from desk work" over the shaft
of the fire engine to stare at Amalia, her sister. On the next day
a messenger brought her a letter in which Sortini summoned
her angrily and in most vulgar terms to come to his bed at
once since he had only half an hour to spare. Amalia, by her
standards so insultingly solicited, tore the letter to pieces and
threw them into the messenger's face.

Amalia's courageous action entailed the ruin of the entire
Barnabas family. Their attempts to apologize to the insulted
servant have been in vain, since he had followed his master
when Sortini "withdrew to more distant departments" in the
Castle, so that after a while people almost forgot his name.
Still trying to find out something about Sortini, Olga has by
now spent two nights a week for two years with the sex-starved
servants of officials in the stable of the *Herrenhof*.

Having lost his position with the fire department, a most
painful loss for him, Amalia's father had also to give up his
flourishing business and work for a former employee. While
spending his free time trying to get help from the Mayor, the
secretaries, the lawyers, and the clerks, he is losing the rest
of his money since all accept bribes only in order to avoid
arguments with him, of course, but do nothing in return. The
Castle hypocritically refuses to recognize the fact that he is
being punished or persecuted, so that the desperate man, in a
last attempt, posts himself next to one of the roads leading to
the Castle, trying to attract the attention of one of the gentlemen
on their way to it. The carriages at that place, the home stretch,
travel with great speed, and yet the deluded petitioner believes
that one of the officials would eventually recognize his Fire
Department badge, now illegitimately worn, stop, and listen
to him. Repeating this insane wait day after day in all kinds
of weather, he contracts a severe case of rheumatism which
cripples him. His wife, who had accompanied him when he
grew too feeble to undergo the daily torture by himself, con-

tracted the same disease. Amalia, of course, does not escape punishment either; patiently she nurses her ailing parents, whose senile infantilism is particularly hard to bear.

Realizing that K. cannot understand the laws and mores of her village, Olga explains calmly, as if speaking to a child about simple natural laws, the "love life" of the officials and of Klamm, the mightiest "lover" of them all!

"Klamm's a kind of commander over women, he orders first one and then another to come to him, puts up with none of them for long, and orders them to go just as he had ordered them to come. Oh, Klamm wouldn't even give himself the trouble of writing a letter first. And in comparison with that is it so monstrous that Sortini, who's so retiring, . . . should condescend for once to write in his beautiful official hand a letter however abominable? . . . There's no such thing as an official's unhappy love affair. . . . We do know that women can't help loving officials once they give them any encouragement; why, they even love them beforehand, let them deny it as much as they like."[27]

And these hilariously satirized employees of Count Westwest are supposed to be "heavenly authorities," or again "life powers which govern everything," with Klamm as a "superpersonal love power!" Only an obsession, to be discussed later, could lead so many Kafka critics to such strange conclusions.

In her account of the Castle officials' erotic Cockaigne Olga also mentions "the great gulf" between an official and a village cobbler's daughter. There is a slight similarity between the contemptuous way in which the official Sortini treats the cobbler's daughter Amalia and the abrupt way in which the official Dr. Kafka broke with the cobbler's daughter Julie Wohryzek. Julie, incidentally, with whom Kafka had planned a prudential marriage, was the physical model for Frieda.

After his long visit with Olga, K. returns to the *Herrenhof*, since Barnabas informs him that Erlanger, one of the first secretaries of Klamm, wishes to see him. Although this is a very important matter for K., he first has a long discussion with Frieda while Jeremias, the assistant, waits impatiently for her in her room. K.'s ex-fiancée has reasons for having broken with him, not the least important being that he visits Olga's outcast

family and returns "with the odor of their room" in his clothes,
an unbearable disgrace for Klamm's former paramour.
Realizing that he has definitely lost Frieda, K. at last wants
to go to Erlanger's room, but cannot find the right door in
the long corridor, and on entering the wrong one awakens the
official Bürgel in his broad bed. K. is invited to sit down on it
and is so overpowered by the desire to sleep that he hardly
realizes the friendly secretary's immediate interest in the case
of the unemployed land-surveyor. It is between four and five
in the morning, and K. is too tired to obey an inner voice which
tells him that what Bürgel had to say was of greatest importance
to him. Sinking deeper and deeper into sleep, he misses the
best chance to bypass all the obstacles which lie in the way
of his being accepted by the Castle. Bürgel warns him: "Pay
attention, there are sometimes, after all, opportunities . . . in
which by means of a word, a glance, a sign of trust, more can
be achieved than by means of lifelong exhausting efforts";[28]
and now he expounds in detail to his sleeping guest an idea
which reappears in the novel for the third time: The Brücken-
kopf landlady had talked to K. about the possibility of achieving
something "in the teeth of every rule and tradition."[29] Olga had
said the evening before that "there must certainly be some
among them [the officials] who had good sympathetic hearts,
which they couldn't give way to in their official capacity, but
out of office hours, if one caught them at the right time, they
would surely listen."[30] When Bürgel now explains what constitutes such an "opportune moment," his explanations fit the
present one in every detail:

"One tends involuntarily to judge things from a more private point
of view at night, the allegations of the applicants take on more
weight than is due to them, the judgment of the case becomes
adulterated with quite irrelevant considerations of the rest of the
applicants' situation, their sufferings and anxieties."[31]

Bürgel then describes how such a lucky situation may occur:
The applicant stumbles upon the wrong office, being overly tired
and the splendid opportunity is offered. If he wants to he can
"dominate everything and to that end has to do nothing but in
some way or other put forward his plea, for which fulfillment

is already waiting."[32] Bürgel's explanations are satirically comical because, taking all angles into consideration, as only a legally trained official can, he says essentially that, surprised by the nocturnal visit of a party, the official may show some humaneness. As in a fairy tale, a little weakness has cost K. his golden opportunity.[33] Fast asleep during Bürgel's explanation, he does not wake up until the secretary Erlanger, whose room is next door, knocks impatiently on the wall and orders him to come out. Erlanger wants him to send Frieda back to the barroom so that Klamm's routine is in no way disturbed. This, given as an order, is a humiliation for K. who, although understanding it as such, is powerless to assert himself before officials.

Staying in the corridor while the documents for the day's work are brought by two servants, K. disturbs the order of the day considerably since the gentlemen cannot leave their rooms because of his presence. "In the morning, so soon after having been asleep, they were too bashful, too vulnerable, to be able to expose themselves to the gaze of strangers, they literally felt, however completed dressed they might be, too naked to show themselves."[34] These and other reproaches about his insensitivity in regard to the officials K. has to accept from the landlord before he is at last allowed to remain in the barroom. After he has slept there for twelve hours, Pepi, the new barmaid replacing Frieda, suggests that he move in with her and her two roommates. He could help them with their work, and he would like it there. She sums up his hopeless position, reminding him that it is cold and that he has neither work nor a bed to sleep in.

At this point, K., utterly defeated, has only two unacceptable ways of surviving in the village: joining the pariah family of Barnabas and becoming an outcast himself, or hiding from the village and the Castle in the maids' chamber, dependent on the girls' discretion. While the landlady of the *Herrenhof* engages K. in an unfriendly conversation about her ample wardrobe which he had criticized, he is almost pulled out of the building by Gerstäcker, the drayman who, a few days ago, had saved the exhausted stranger because he did not want him to remain in front of his house. Although K. does not know anything about horses, Gerstäcker wants to hire him as groom

for room and board. To K.'s blunt reply that the old man only
wants him to influence the official Erlanger in his favor, the
drayman answers: "Certainly, what interest should I have in
you otherwise?" To continue his tenuous claim to life in the
village, K. will have to pretend before the villagers to be
Gerstäcker's stable groom, and before Gerstäcker that he has
some influence with Erlanger, who had simply ordered him to
send Frieda back to serve Klamm his beer.

The fragment ends with the hero in this wretched situation.
When asked by Brod how the novel was to end, Kafka told him:

He was not to relax in his struggle, but was to die worn out by it.
Round his deathbed the villagers were to assemble, and from the
Castle itself the word was to come that though K.'s legal claim
to live in the village was not valid, yet, taking certain auxiliary
circumstances into account, he was to be permitted to live and
work there.[35]

IV   The Castle Above the Clouds

It is certain that the bureaucrats finally kill the hero with
their war of attrition, including their little jokes. As has already
been stated, the combination of jocularity and cruelty in the
bureaucratic circles of that time was well known. An example
which must have impressed Kafka was the fun that Austrian
officials had with ignorant, helpless Jews who, in 1787, by the
decree of Emperor Joseph II of Austria, had to have German
surnames and were given by the witty officials such opprobrious
and ludicrous ones as Eselskopf (Donkey head), Goldlust (Lust
for Gold), Edelstein (Jewel), Diamant (Diamond).

Whenever Kafka mentions officials in his diaries, letters, or
previous works he ridicules them or shows contempt; his own
weaknesses he called Beamtenlaster ("vices of a bureaucrat").
As mentioned above, he considered modern history ridiculous
because it consisted for the greatest part of "negotiations of
officials." He did not believe in the world-redeeming power of
Russian Communism since "the revolution evaporates leaving
behind only the mud of a new bureaucracy; the fetters of tor-
mented mankind are made of red tape."[36] A little over a year
before he started work on Das Schloss, he called the Workers'

Accident Insurance Company *ein dunkles Bürokratennest* ("a
dark nest of bureaucrats").[37] *Bürokratennest,* a common term
in German, may well have been a germinal metaphor for the
castle which looks like a conglomeration of little houses "gath-
ered" together (*zusammengetragen*) on top of the castle hill.
Zusammentragen ("to gather together") fits the building of a
nest much better than the building of a castle. Also the chief
bureaucrat Klamm, the "screaming eagle," has his eyrie up
there on the castle hill.

How Kafka could have chosen bureaucrats as the objective
correlative for K.'s so-called pilgrimage, his heavenly quest, and
his searching for Grace, is very difficult to see, but that he
should have satirized them as the implacable enemies of the
luckless K.s is plausible even though the religious school has
declared such an interpretation anathema.

In his epilogue to the first edition of *Das Schloss* (1926),
Brod laid the foundation for religious, allegorical interpretations
of the novel; they are by now far more numerous than psychoanalytical, Marxian, and, certainly, literary ones. Brod as interpreter raised the Castle from the "specifically Jewish" to the
"general human" and, finally, to the "general religious" level.[38]
During this ascent, he casts a short glance at Goethe's *Faust*.
Because, on his deathbed, the dying K. receives permission to
live and work in the village, Brod feels encouraged to say:

With this reminiscence (very remote and, ironically, reduced to a
minimum) of the passage in Goethe's *Faust* "Whoe'r strives unweariedly is not beyond redeeming" this novel which one may
call Franz Kafka's *Faust* was to end. Of course, it is a *Faust* in an
intentionally modest, even poor attire and with the essential modifica-
tion that this Faust is not driven by yearning for the ultimate goals
and insights of man, but the desire for the most primitive pre-
requisites which existence requires, for taking root through his work
and a home in a human community.[39]

The modest though basic ambitions of K. fit into the small
town, "where Gretchen loved and suffered" and which Faust
passed through. What distinguishes Faust from the legion of
fictitious characters who strive unweariedly for life's humble

goals is his heroic *Entgrenzungstrieb*—the urge to break down all limitations set up by God, nature, or man.

Ascending to the religious level, Brod expounds in the same epilogue: "This Castle . . . is exactly what theologians call 'Grace,' the divine guidance of human fate (of the village). . . . In *Der Prozess* and *Das Schloss* the two forms in which the deity is manifested (as the cabala understands it)—Judgment and Grace are represented."[40]

Repeating Brod's ideas, Thomas Mann gave them added importance in a short commentary called "Homage" which prefaces the English translation of *Das Schloss*: "In the sardonic dreamsymbolism of the novel the village represents life, the soil, the community, healthy normal existence, and the blessings of human and bourgeois society. The Castle, on the other hand, represents the divine dispensation, the state of grace—puzzling, remote, incomprehensible."[41]

By their united efforts, Brod and Mann lifted the Castle above the clouds, and there it remained. Who could seriously doubt Brod, the intimate friend of the author he knew best, or Mann, who had written brilliant essays on literary topics? That Kafka seldom spoke about his works even with Brod, and that Brod reported all these conversations, was disregarded as much as the fact that Mann had merely repeated Brod's ideas. Anagoge, the allegorizing method which elevates the literal meaning of a text to spiritual heights, prevailed. Henceforth many Kafka commentators felt the same repugnance at understanding their canonic author's texts *realiter* (i.e., in their literal sense) which educated ancients felt when reading Homer without allegorical commentary, or which educated Christians of the first centuries felt when confronted with the anthropomorphisms and secular passages of the Old Testament. In his *Confessions*, St. Augustine declares that the catholic faith appeared much more acceptable to his reason "especially," as he says, "after I heard some passages of the Old Testament by whose literal meaning I was slain [*occidebar*] resolved figuratively [allegorically]."[42]

By the same old method, the ludicrous but also contemptible officials were "resolved figuratively," and reappeared as "an inscrutable hierarchy" (Brod) or as "heavenly authorities"

(Mann). The following examples are taken only from books written by authors well known to specialists in the Kafka-field. In the most theologically oriented work we read of K.'s superior Klamm, the head of department X, that he "(like Yahweh) must not be called by his name."[43] In the novel, this commandment responds to the landlady's simple request that K. should not use Klamm's name all the time, since it makes her nervous. Other critics as well discovered supernatural beings in *Das Schloss*. To one of them, the Virginia smoking, beer-drinking, much copulating Klamm appears as a character of "absolute transcendence" and then again of "immense transcendence."[44] Another enraptured commentator calls him "the powerful one whose love is an expression of his strength, power and glory,"[45] almost using the language of *The Lord's Prayer*.

Contrary to the author's intention, the protagonist, as most critics see him, has various sublime goals. He is striving "for knowledge, perhaps some fierce progress of the soul, a saving relationship with universal powers, however mad."[46] It is hard to imagine Klamm, Galater, Erlanger, and the other bureaucrats as providers of knowledge or saviors of anybody's soul.

After the divine powers have become universal powers, the Castle comes closer to earth, although it is still high up in the air: "Kafka has found in K.'s antagonist, the Castle, the perfect image to conceal his own uncertainties about man's ultimate destiny and yet to manifest in K.'s meandering through this labyrinth his incessant longing for a certainty of one kind or the other."[47] Neither Kafka nor K. ever inquire about man's "ultimate destiny."

Finally there appeared a moral interpretation in the last book so far which gives an exegesis of most of Kafka's works:

The Castle is . . . one big parable about the impossibility of uniting the villages of life with the castle of thinking-about-life; it is a lesson to K. in the reality of the world. But at the very same time, and with equal force, K. is a lesson to the world in morality: the novel is a parable about the unavailing struggle of man which he, nevertheless, must not and cannot give up to spiritualize the world-reality and thereby liberate it.[48]

Officials, however, are the executive power while the spirit is the legislative power, the creative force. K. is not spiritualizing anything; he is fighting with bureaucrats who have all the power to play with him while he struggles for the right to live and work where necessity forces him to.

Brod also assigned to Sortini a divine role, an interpretation which was supported by most critics till the mid-sixties. Kafka, no inexperienced wanderer in the maze of Eros, satirizes in the Sortini episode the Puritan who, when overcome by libido, becomes angry with his own body and insults the woman who has aroused him. Brod, disregarding this fact of life, comments:

> The Sortini episode is directly parallel to Kierkegaard's book [*Fear and Trembling*] which has as its starting point that God asks of Abraham even a crime, the sacrifice of his child, and in which this paradox helps to elucidate the triumphant assertion that ethical and religious categories are not congruous.[49]

Apart from the mislabeling the sacrifice of the firstborn in biblical times a crime, he erroneously recognizes ideas from *Fear and Trembling* in this scene. Brod's interpretation was accepted by, among others, Camus who, as can easily be shown, did not read *Das Schloss* very carefully.

Even where the vicious little man is not granted divine honors, he still dwells in lonely heights: "... Sortini is the guarantor of the spiritual world, indeed is the spiritual world itself. That is the meaning of the sentence: that all women always have to love officials, even if they do not know it."[50]

The desire to anagogize Sortini is so strong that a critic may say the direct opposite of what the author does. The Sortini episode begins with the din of ineptly blown trumpets with which the Castle has presented the fire department. This cater-wauling, which one commentator calls "angelic and satanic sounds," indicates "that a moment of great importance is at hand and prepares the reader for the meeting of the human and the more-than-human."[51] The meeting begins with Sortini's jumping over the shaft of the fire engine "with his legs stiff from desk-work" in order to have a better look at Amalia. A less-than-human meeting in bed for which he craves does not take place. The critic continues: "Nor can we overlook the suggestively ambiguous central image, the fire engine, which is really a big water squirter [*Feuerspritze*]. . . . Keeping close to the Castle's gift, the phallic fire engine, Sortini refuses to mingle with the crowd."[52] Actually the word *Feuerspritze* which Kafka uses is the German word for fire engine, and Sortini's need for detumescence is obvious; it does not have to be explained by phallic symbols.

Included in Kafka's satire on bureaucracy is a satire on the *petit bourgeois*, the loyal *Untertan* ("subject"), represented by the none-too-bright father of Amalia. Old Barnabas is as proud of his badge as old Samsa is of his gold-embroidered porter's cap. Both these fathers and Old Rossmann suffer deeply because the family escutcheon has been blotted, and Samsa as well as Rossmann react with bourgeois cruelty against their prodigals.

Kafka's subtle satires of the bourgeoisie in his early works did not remain completely unnoticed, it seems. When Carl Sternheim in 1915 received the Fontane Prize he gave the prize money, which he, the rich son of a banker, did not need, to the little-known author of "Die Verwandlung" and "Der Heizer." Sternheim's fame had been established by the merciless comedies in which he had attacked the *Spiesser* ("Babbits") of the Wilhelminian era: officials, nouveaux riches, social climbers, crawling *Untertanen* ("subjects"). Sympathy with young Kafka's bourgeois satire seems to be the only plausible explanation for Sternheim's choice. It is strange that Brod did not acknowledge in his friend, the writer, what he described as a strong characteristic of the man who, according to him, was "admittedly limitlessly skeptical and ironic."[53]

The critics' religious *Luftschloss* ("the castle in the air," in Spain) appears on the cover of a 1974 reprint of *The Castle*: A rock of tremendous dimensions, with a castle on top, hovers in the air; it is a reproduction of René Magritte's *Chateau des Pyrénées*. This rock "easily suggests" the uplifting interpretations of *Das Schloss*.

CHAPTER 10

The Last Metamorphoses

I Hunger Artist and Dog Metaphysician

WHEN Kafka started work on his last novel, he had less than two and a half years to live. His physicians gave him hope, but the four stories he wrote during this time are all retrospective, their four heroes—a hunger artist, an old dog, a badger, and a mouse—are approaching the end of their lives which consisted of futile efforts.

In the spring of 1922 he wrote the first of these terminal works: "Ein Hungerkünstler" ("A Hunger Artist"). Even though this story never received such detailed and overt praise from its author as "Das Urteil," it was indirectly singled out by Kafka as the work of his last creative period which had his full approval. Without Brod's prodding or even knowledge, he sent it to *Die Neue Rundschau*, the most representative German literary magazine, where it appeared in October, 1922. The story was not only exempt from the annihilation he had decreed in his "last Will" for most of his works; he himself had it printed again as the title story of his last book.

The hero, a hunger artist,[1] on exhibit in various towns, is attracting many people, until the interest in this kind of spectacle wanes, and he is forced to dismiss his impresario and hire himself out to a circus, where in his cage, he is on exhibition as part of the side show. While in happier days his main sorrow had been the impresario's strictly imposed limit of forty hunger days, he is now unhappy about the general indifference toward him. He has been without food for an incredibly long time, but nobody counts the days, and the circus visitors hurry past his cage to see the wild animals.

The forgotten man lies dying on his straw when an overseer and some roustabouts looking for a cage find him. With his

164

last breath, the pitiful bundle of bones whispers into the over-seer's ear the tragic discovery he has made at the end of his life. He explains the real reason for his fasting:

". . . because I couldn't find the food I liked. If I had found it, believe me, I should have made no fuss and stuffed myself like you or anyone else." These were his last words, but in his dimming eyes remained the firm though no longer proud persuasion that he was still continuing to fast.[2]

Like most Kafka heroes, he realized too late the futility of his life. The crowds had come to admire the hero with the iron will who could do what no other man could do so well: conquer man's grim enemy—hunger. What they saw, however, was a sick freak.

Again Kafka had anticipated the unwritten work in related metaphors; but in the case of "Ein Hungerkünstler" such metaphors are found in his writings from the beginning. In 1903 he assures Oskar Pollak: "Playing the hermit is disgusting . . . ; it is better to bite into life instead of one's tongue."[3] In 1912, the year of his breakthrough as a writer, he described himself as a hunger artist, using a similar metaphor: "When it became clear in my organism that writing was the most productive direction for my being to take, everything rushed in that direction and left empty all those abilities which were directed toward the joys of sex, eating, drinking, philosophical reflection and above all music. *I atrophied in all these directions*"[4] (italics mine).

The hunger artist's tragic understanding that his uniqueness is not greatness was also experienced by Kafka, though in a much weaker form. Kafka complained that he always stood aside, never accepted life's invitations to participate. "I used to consider this refusal a good sign," he writes in 1921, "(misled by the vague great hopes I cherished for myself). Today only a remnant of this benevolent interpretation remains."[5] In "Ein Hungerkünstler" and his last story, "Josephine, die Sängerin" ("Josephine, the Singer") that remnant, too, had disappeared.

No other Kafka story is so intimately connected with his autobiographical statements of which those quoted are only a small selection. And yet, there seems to have existed a more optimistic countercurrent in his life during the last two years, manifested also in his being able to enter into a real love relation with a woman. It finds expression in isolated hopeful statements like the following, antedating the "Hungerkünstler": ". . . straight on only, starved beast, lies the road to food that will sustain you, air that you can breathe, a free life, even if it should take you beyond life."[6] The food and air metaphors belong together; their combination with the desired freedom shows how close they are to the work written shortly thereafter.

"Ein Hungerkünstler" has a Fortinbras ending. After the hunger artist has been buried, a young leopard who, in his beauty and vitality, contrasts with his wretched predecessor, is put into the empty cage. "He lacked nothing," while the dead man tragically lacked everything that is required for a radiant life.

The leopard as well as his predecessor in the cage, the hunger artist, have badly confused the critics who did not know about their function, as far as the realistic aspect of the story goes. Hence such strange statements as the following: "An artist has recourse to attracting attention by starvation after his impresario has lost interest in him."[7] "He [Kafka] concentrates the sentence 'Artists starve,' into the Hunger-Artist."[8] The word *Hungerkünstler* is misunderstood. The word *Künstler* by itself means artist, but in compounds it designates performers in the circus or in a variety show like *Trapezkünstler* ("trapeze artist") or *Entkleidungskünstlerin* ("stripper"), both of whom display skills but are not artists. Besides, Kafka never concerned himself with the artist and his relation to society. The entire story is considered an allegory of the supposed cultural decline in the modern world which prefers displays of brute vitality (the leopard) to the refined enjoyments the artist has to offer.

The religious school of criticism offers equations like the following: hunger artist—saint, prophet, glorification of asceticism, criticism of asceticism; the impresario—organized religion with its delight in pomp or the theatrical. The German word *Panther* ("leopard") has been translated incorrectly as "panther," which means to Americans and many Britons the big black cat, "hence" something evil. Although Kafka wrote a prose poem about a beautiful leopard, an equal to Rilke's famous quatrains "Der

Panther," the critics make the big cat a villain. The "panther" is supposed to be an allegory of the animal nature of man, of sensualism, or even of the "philistine who has supplanted the saint in modern society, . . . the businessman, that healthy beast of prey."[9]

Emphatically two noted critics maintain in their commentaries on the leopard that Kafka despised nature. The main reason for the hunger artist's profession is in the one critic's opinion "his violent aversion to the food offered to man, which his nature is demanding. The leopard, nature's healthy representative, devours his scraps of meat with relish. And one may—and probably must—extend the hunger artist's violent disgust for food to the disgust for the entire sensuous nature of man."[10] Soon after this first philosophically founded attack on Kafka's leopard, there followed a second one of the same kind. Seeing in "Ein Hunger-künstler" an allegorical tale of the conflict between spirit and nature, this critic concludes: "But who remains unconvincible anyhow and prefers the leopard to the hunger artist has regressed to that alienated animalistic world which Kafka tried to unhinge."[11] No critic ever "preferred" the leopard. The Judaic author of the prose poem about the young animal reveals the strong influence the "pagan" Goethe had on his feelings, particularly during his last years. After having watched not a leopard, but mussels, limpets, and crabs on the beach, Goethe felt and thought: "How enchanting, how glorious such a living creature is! How wonderfully adapted to its state of existence, how true, how real [*seiend*]!"[12]

While the interpretations of the religious school can be severely doubted, there is no doubt possible about a profound mistake which doomed to error almost all commentaries on "Forschungen eines Hundes" ("Investigations of a Dog"). Kafka wrote this fragment of forty-six pages in the summer of 1922 while visiting his sister Ottla in the country where he, incidentally, took walks with the dog of the farm.

The reader who is familiar with Kafka's diary will recognize the author in the hero of the story, the old philosophizing dog who characterizes himself as ". . . solitary and withdrawn, with nothing to occupy me save my hopeless but, as far as I am concerned, indispensable little investigations, that is how I live. . . . The others treat me with respect but do not understand my way of life; yet they bear me no grudge, and even young dogs . . . do not deny me a reverential greeting."[13] Shortly after the hero has introduced himself in this fashion, he makes a significant statement which explains the element of alienation in this story and points to its meaning: "Indeed when I reflect on it—and I have time and disposition and capacity enough for that—I see that dogdom is in every way a marvelous institution. Apart from us dogs there are all sorts of creatures in the world, wretched, limited, dumb creatures who have no language but certain cries. . . ."[14]

The critics have, almost without exception, disregarded the all-important words "Apart from us dogs." This dog knows only inferior animals, but does not know that there are human beings in the world. Kafka repeats this crucial point frequently. For example, about a page farther down the dog states: "No creatures to my knowledge live in such wide dispersion as we dogs, . . . engaged in strange vocations that are often incomprehensible even to our canine neighbors, holding firmly to laws that are not those of the dog world, but are actually directed against it."[15] Those laws come from man and are against the instinctive desires of the dogs who are just as ignorant about the real powers dominating them as their pensive brother. He alone, however, is plagued by futile reflections and inner unrest about "a profound error" which he suspects without ever being able to understand it.

As a young dog the hero of the story had had an experience which became important for all his later life, making a philosopher of him, and starting him on his tireless quest for truth about the canine world, to him the highest form of life on this earth. Roving at night through the countryside, he all of a sudden encountered a bright morning (the lighted tent in which a variety show takes place). Suddenly there appeared before his eyes seven dogs which did unbelievable things (they are trained animals in a dog act). He does not understand any of the surrounding circumstances: the terrible sounds accompanying the strange fellow dogs (applause), the music they conjure up out of empty space (the accompanying orchestra). This music drives him into a jumble of wooden sticks (the legs of the spectators' chairs). He knew at that time "almost nothing of the creative gift for music with which the canine race alone is endowed."[16] This is again a clear statement of his basic error, but, worst of all, he sensed that the dogs were acting under coercion (their trainer), but he could not see who coerced them. This mysterious experience keeps him occupied for a long time. Later he reflects on the wisdom of the ancestors: "Wet everything [Urinate on everything] as much as you can." He ponders: "The earth needs our water to nourish it and only at that price provides us with our food, the emergence of which, however, and this should not be forgotten, can also be hastened by certain spells, songs, and movements."[17]

Doomed to ignorance about metaphysical questions like this dog, man has tried, through the ages, to influence unknown powers through his rituals. Kafka's religious faith, his belief in an absolute which he called "the indestructible" did not include dogmas and rituals.

All the details of "Forschungen" "fall into place" if the basic error of the quester dog is kept in mind. The *Lufthunde* ("aerial dogs"), for example, assumed by the other dogs to *be* artists and philosophers, by the critics to *represent* bohemians, artists, and even "symbols of a realm that is inherent in the earthly world and that is at the same time unearthly"[18] are pampered lap dogs, which their mistresses carry in their arms. The Kafka dogs, however, see them hovering in the air.

Other problems prove unsolvable to the dog. Where does the food come from which strangely appears in the air (if man holds it up) or on the ground (when put in a bowl)? Thus the old country dog pursues, in the simplicity of his unspoiled soul, metaphysical speculations, predestined to be errors, because of a blind spot which, as Kafka sees it, metaphysicians possess.

II Death and Testament

In the summer of 1922, Kafka stopped working on "Forschungen," and in the first week of the following September he gave up finishing *Das Schloss* after futile attempts "to connect" with the fragment. His letters reveal how bleakly unhappy he was in the unproductive months which followed, until in July,

1923, he accompanied his sister Elli to Müritz at the Baltic
Sea. Near his hotel was a vacation camp of the Berlin Jewish
People's Home at which Felice had taught for a while. In this
children's camp he met, as one of the helpers, Dora Diamant,
a nineteen-year-old girl who had left her Chassidic home in
Poland. In his first letter to Brod, Kafka reveals his love for
the young girl, whom he had only met a few days earlier: "She
is charming—a really strong individuality, genuineness, seriousness, a childlike lovable seriousness [*eine kindlich liebe Ernst-
haftigkeit*]."[19] The German adjective *lieb* only approximately
equals "lovable," just as *kindlich* is more than childlike. After
his fleeting Tristan experience with the Swiss girl, Kafka had
never again, in his diaries and letters, written so lovingly about,
or to, a woman. What he had felt about Felice and Milena had
been admiration, not love. Dora was nineteen at that time, Kafka
had just turned forty; but Dora loved the doomed man with
all her youthful passion and devotion, and Kafka responded
with love, not with a worshipful correspondence. Felice had
talked about furniture; Dora read him the royal verses of Isaiah.
A good Hebraist, in spite of her youth, she helped her lover
with his studies of that ancient language, told him about her
Chassidic past, and listened with fascination when he read to
her from his own works and those of his favorite writers. He
also introduced her, a more than willing student, to Western
culture. In his letter to Brod, he quotes one of her revealing
remarks: "It is strange how one takes over the views of a loved
human being even if they contradict one's own previous ideas."[20]

Kafka was a changed man; he broke with Prague, moved with
Dora to Steglitz, a suburb of Berlin, into a small apartment where
his prized solitude was not possible and never missed. Dora
reports how he liked her to stay with him while he wrote and
how, at times, sitting on the sofa she fell asleep when he
worked very late. Obviously the millstones of his torture mill
had stopped grinding. When the landlady, unwilling to tolerate
mere lovers in her house, told them to move out, the otherwise
nervous and irritable man took the inconvenience in good humor
and wrote a short sketch about the irate mistress of the house
entitled "Eine kleine Frau" ("A Little Woman"). What Dora
did for Kafka, whose health was continuously deteriorating, he

expressed in his last letter to Milena: "... as for the rest I am well and tenderly sheltered here to the limits of earthly possibilities."[21]

This shelter inspired in part the narrative "Der Bau" ("The Burrow") in which a badger tries skillfully but in vain to escape the deadly enemy who is bound to find and kill him. About a year before he wrote the story, Kafka anticipated the metaphor by comparing himself to "a desperate animal in its burrow, enemies everywhere";[22] but these enemies had been merely noisy children in front of his window. He dreamed of escaping to Palestine with Dora as soon as his health would permit; he wanted to marry her in spite of parental opposition on both sides, but it was too late.

In April he had to return to Prague. His tuberculosis had worsened in the cold winter, and due to the privations of the inflation, which had reached enormous proportions in 1923. Soon after, tuberculosis of the larynx was diagnosed, and Kafka was given only a few more months to live, a death sentence which neither the physicians nor Dora nor Klopstock told the moribund patient. Klopstock, a medical student, had become his devoted friend while working in the sanatorium Matliar in the Tatra mountains, where Kafka spent ten months in 1920–1921. Interrupting his medical studies shortly before the examinations, Klopstock accompanied Kafka and Dora to the sanatorium Kierling, near Vienna, to assist his dying friend.

Without his usual distrust of physicians, Kafka now obeyed his doctors; his masochistic willingness to be annihilated had gone. When the attending specialist, trying to cheer him up, told him that his larynx looked better, he embraced Dora and cried with joy. This supposed religious ascetic, this supposed Manichaean despiser of reality craved to the last the few lovely gifts life still held for him: the fragrance of lilac and ripe strawberries, the hand of a loving woman on his forehead.

Since he was supposed to speak as little as possible, he wrote his thoughts and needs during the last days on slips of paper. Among them there is only one expressing a religious feeling: "Into the depth, into the deep harbor."[23] The concept of depth appears now and then in entries like the following of 1916: "Receive me into your arms, they are the depths, receive me

into the depths; if you refuse me now, then later."²⁴ But the
slip with the sigh *de profundis* is the exception. Where his
jottings do not deal with sickroom matters they speak of life
and its pleasures. Even the "leopard" motif appeared once more
in the thoughts of the moribund author of "Ein Hungerkünstler":

"My cousin, he was a magnificent man. When this Robert, he was
then about forty already, ... had a lot to do, what with his work
and his pleasures ... when he used to come to the bathing establishment Sophia, threw off his clothes with a few flicks of the hand,
jumped into the water and threshed around in it *with the strength
of a beautiful wild animal,* gleaming from the water, with his eyes
sparkling, and then was off again like a shot toward the weir—
that was magnificent" (italics mine).²⁵

A few days before his death, the proofs of the book *Ein
Hungerkünstler* arrived, and Kafka began his last activity as
a writer with a heavy heart, not only because of his debilitated
condition but also because, as the conversation slip says, this
reading would "excite him too much," since he "had to experience it anew." After he had read proof for a while, Klopstock
saw him in tears; it was not the first but the last time that he
was so deeply moved by one of his works. "Ich muss es doch
von neuem erleben"²⁶ ("After all, I must experience it ["Ein
Hungerkünstler"] anew") is the last of the many comments
Kafka made about his work. Also "Ein Hungerkünstler" is neither
parable nor allegory. These genres cannot be "experienced anew,"
and certainly would never make their author weep. The general
truth which a parable expresses appeals to the intellect, not to
the feelings. Kafka did write some parables, but his stories
and novels deal with complex feelings and were not written to
illustrate religious or philosophical maxims. To the end, the
commentator Kafka speaks about having written his "inner
biography."

On the last day of his life, Monday, June 2, he wrote a long
letter to his parents, a document of filial love and a brave attempt
to keep them from worrying about the state of his health. At
twelve o'clock at night he fell asleep; four hours later, on June 3,
his agony began. Impatiently he demanded a lethal dose of
morphine, but received only enough to relieve his pains. Mis-

taking Klopstock, who bent over him, for his sister Elli he said: "Go, Elli, not so close, not so close," and when Klopstock straightened up he was satisfied. Then he lost consciousness. In 1914 Kafka's parents had found a fine apartment for him and Felice, his wife to be, and Kafka remarked in his diary: "I wonder whether they will lay me in my grave too, after a life made happy by their solicitude."[27] They did.

In Kafka literature, frequent references are made to a testament according to which he wanted his manuscripts burned and existing books not reprinted. This "testament" consisted of two slips of paper in the drawer of Kafka's desk which was filled with the sediment of years. The later of these slips was written early in 1922 when Kafka was deeply depressed since he expected to die of a threatening pneumonia. In his last story, "Josefine, die Sängerin, oder das Volk der Mäuse" ("Josephine the Singer, or the Mouse Folk"), written in 1923, the author represented himself as a female mouse among the nation of mice (the Jews), as their singer, a little helpless mouse which cannot even whistle as loud as the other mice. Ridiculing his role as poet laureate of his people, he finishes his story about little Josephine: "Josephine, redeemed from the earthly sorrows . . . will rise to the heights of redemption and be forgotten like all her brothers."[28]

Then Kafka wanted the "heightened redemption" of being completely forgotten? The author of "Josefine" remained a man of indecision to the end; he dealt with the testament as he dealt with other communications whose results he wanted and did not want. He had warned Felice's father about his future son-in-law in a letter he sent to Felice, who never delivered it; the long letter in which he accuses his father was sent to his mother, who never delivered it; the "testament" decreeing the annihilation of his manuscripts was addressed to Max Brod, the man least likely to obey him in this matter, the most unreliable executor.

CHAPTER 11

Conclusion: Kafka's Apotheosis

THE first interpreter using simply literary criticism when commenting on Kafka's works was Kafka himself. He had no followers, but, as previously discussed, modern critics censured him because his explanations entailed a loss of "universal meaning." This is, however, only one of the many paradoxes in Kafka criticism, which is rich in paradoxes, the greatest of these being the role played by Max Brod.

With a lifelong friend's best intentions, Brod gave the critics the false alarm of which it is said in "Ein Landarzt" that if you follow it once "you will never set things straight again." He gave it early, in an article in *Die Neue Rundschau*, published in 1921, which was entitled "Franz Kafka," but which should have had the subtitle *Franciscus Seraphicus* because it contains heavenly metaphors like the following:[1] "Visions of immeasurable depth . . . a melody which does not consist of earthly matters." Certain characters in Kafka's stories, according to Brod, "carry the sweetness of redemption," and there is in his work "a smile in the vicinity of the ultimate things, a metaphysical smile." In the same article Brod raised the humble family man in "Die Sorge des Hausvaters," loosely translated "The Cares of a Family Man," to a "heavenly family man." This strange celestial father-figure was to be followed by many others with whom the Kafka critics populated their allegorical heavens.

What Brod has to say about *Der Prozess* reveals the goal behind his partly ridiculous hyperboles: When reading *Der Prozess* he felt as if he were "reading the few supreme masterpieces of world literature. This book fills the space of the world. . . . An invisible celestial sphere hovers over this book as over Kafka's entire work." Brod, the superb manager of his friend's fame, wanting him to be counted among the immortals of literature, was driven by love and admiration to gather *Vorschusslorbeer* ("advance laurels") for him. It may therefore be assumed that he unconsciously tried to compensate for the

174

translation: "The category of sacredness." Brod repeated the vague term using a synonym: *das Heilige*. "A characteristic which placed him in the category of the sacred [*die Kategorie des Heiligen*][9] was his absolute faith ... in a world of rightness, in the indestructible. ..." There is nothing vague in the translations of this passage, which are real howlers. The *Miscellany* places Kafka "in the category of saints,"[10] and in the book-length version he is squeezed into "the category of a saint." Trying to weaken the impact of his hagiographic statements, Brod caused added confusion by admitting that his friend was not "a perfect saint," but a man who "trod the path leading to that ultimate state."[11] The sloppy phrase "not a perfect saint" seems to refer to Kafka's love affairs, but is not intended to be understood that way.

To show the broad range of Kafka criticism it might be mentioned that the evolving saint of Brod is to another critic a devil, a modern devil, of course, a pre-Nazi: "Stated in political terms, his [Kafka's] dilemma was that he could not become a fascist. Not its cruelty but its apparent denial of individualism prevented [*sic*]."[12] There was also the time barrier: "His [Kafka's] had been the prototype of the German personality. But he was forced to wander into death and madness alone. For Hitler had not yet offered the fantasy of a fantasy in his confraternity of the doomed. ..."[13] The *Franz Kafka Miscellany*, on the other hand, has a subtitle, syntactically disconnected like a cry: *Pre-Fascist Exile*.

These aberrations were too obvious to influence later critics, but Brod's exaggerations had given Kafka criticism the direction which the majority of interpreters followed, even though individually they often criticized Brod as editor and commentator of Kafka's works. The spell was too strong to break.

The religious school was not the first to show extraliterary interest in the mysterious author. With Milena's translation of "Der Heizer" and her acquaintance with the Czech Communist writer Stanislav Neumann began the first short contact between Kafka and the world of communism. The second followed almost forty years later, again in his homeland, where a section of the Czech Academy of Sciences, in conjunction with Prague University, too optimistic about "the thaw" in the relations with Russia, convened in Liblice to celebrate the eightieth anniversary

of Kafka's birth by discussing his works from the Marxist point
of view.

Although the celebrated author denied ever having taken
his own generation to task,[14] it was discovered in Liblice that
such criticism was one of his main motives. Talking about the
first impression Kafka had made on him and his generation about
thirty years ago, one speaker reminisced: "We became acquainted
with him at that time as a writer who, with the insistence of
a master with great persuasive force, bared the rot and the
inhumaneness of the capitalist order."[15] That, in essence, is the
praise Kafka's works encountered in the speeches of the Liblice
conference as far as they appeared in the German version of
the proceedings. In the prologue to this book, the hope is
expressed that publications of Kafka's works will soon appear
in Czechoslovakia, and, summing up the result of the conference,
the unnamed author of the prologue states confidently: "Kafka's
return to his native town Prague was not only proclaimed, but
is actually taking place."[16] It did not. The scholars were silenced—
and "little mother Prague," who did not want the German Jew,
wanted "the defeatist bourgeois" even less.

That settled the Kafka problem in the East; but in the West
it is still unsettled, as was shown by the controversies at the
International Symposium in Commemoration of the fiftieth anniversary of Kafka's death at Temple University in 1974. But
Kafka is still being read in Western countries by readers who
do not know any of the more than six thousand five hundred
publications which have appeared about him so far. Of course,
the modern reader cannot learn from him "the right way," just
as he cannot learn how to live in his time and world from T. S.
Eliot, Shakespeare, Dante, or Homer. Kafka's works do not
express ideas but his feelings of insecurity and guilt, which in
the decades since his apotheosis in the twenties have become
the essence of our *Lebensgefühl* in the West. And yet, he is not
literature's grand negativist, nihilist, or penitential homilist.
Besides the delight in his humor and grotesque imagination
the unbiased reader will experience in Kafka's works two
inseparable characteristics of great literature: stylistic perfection
and inner truth.

Notes and References

Abbreviations

A   *America*, translated by Willa and Edwin Muir (New York: Schocken Books, 1974).

B   Max Brod, *Franz Kafka: A Biography*, translated by G. Humphrey Roberts (New York: Schocken Books, 1960).

Br   *Briefe, 1902–1924* (New York: Schocken Books, 1958).

C   *The Castle*, translated by Willa and Edwin Muir, with additional materials translated by Eithne Wilkins and Ernst Kaiser (New York: The Modern Library, 1969).

CS   *Franz Kafka: The Complete Stories*, edited by Nahum N. Glatzer (New York: Schocken Books, 1972).

D-I *The Diaries of Franz Kafka, 1910–1913*, translated by Joseph Kresh (New York: Schocken Books, 1949).

D-II *The Diaries of Franz Kafka, 1914–1923*, translated by Martin Greenberg, with the cooperation of Hannah Arendt (New York: Schocken Books, 1949).

DF   *Dearest Father: Stories and Other Writings*, translated by Ernst Kaiser and Eithne Wilkins (New York: Schocken Books, 1954).

J   Gustav Janouch, *Conversations with Kafka*, translated by Goronwy Rees (New York: New Directions, 1971).

LF   *Letters to Felice*, edited by Erich Heller and Jürgen Born, translated by James Stern and Elisabeth Duckworth (New York: Schocken Books, 1973).

LM   *Letters to Milena*, translated by Tania and James Stern (London: Secker & Warburg, 1953).

T   *The Trial*, translated by Willa and Edwin Muir. Revised and with additional materials translated by E. M. Butler (New York: The Modern Library, 1956).

Note: The date of a diary entry or a letter accompanies the page reference wherever possible.

Chapter One

1. DF 140–41.
2. DF 161.
3. DF 172.
4. DF 174.

5. D-I 286–87, May 4, 1913.
6. J 80.
7. DF 181.
8. Decree of the President of the Republic, Oct. 18, 1945, Annex 12.
9. Ernst Haeckel, *Die Welträtsel*, pp. 423–24.
10. D-I 228, Feb. 4, 1912.
11. Walter Jens, *Ein Jude namens Kafka*, p. 193.
12. LF 42, Nov. 15, 1912. As Flaubert's "spiritual child" he borrowed the technique of making as little use as possible of the narrator as commentator. And if he did not already believe "inner truth" to be the basic criterion of writing, then Flaubert certainly strengthened that idea in him. In his last letter to George Sand, written in 1876, the year of her death, Flaubert passionately discusses his aesthetic credo as a novelist: "As for revealing my personal opinions of the characters I bring on to the stage: no, no,—a thousand times no." In the same letter he emphatically declares: "*For the moment a thing is true, it is good.*" (John Charles Tarver, *Gustave Flaubert as seen in his Works and Correspondence*, p. 228).
13. LF 453, May 6, 1915.
14. D-I, Oct. 14, 1911.
15. Max Brod, *Streitbares Leben*, pp. 66–67.
16. B 168–69.
17. LF 414, May 24, 1914.
18. LM 144.
19. Franz Kafka, *Erzählungen*, p. 301.

Chapter Two

1. DF 163.
2. Br 37, Aug. 1907.
3. Br 49, Oct. 8, 1907.
4. Br 48, Oct. 8, 1907.
5. Br 58, June 9, 1908.
6. B 116. A photograph in Brod's book *Der Prager Kreis* (The Prague Circle), facing p. 49, shows Kafka and Hansi with a dog between them which they both caress. With Hansi cut off, this photograph became popular in books on Kafka and finally, with the dog cut off, Kafka's face retouched, and different clothing sketched in, the Hansi lover and lover of dogs was changed into a hater of Hansis, dogs, and men on the dust jacket of Nahum N. Glatzer's book *I am a Memory Come Alive*.
7. LM 163.

8. Br 59, Sept. 1908.
9. Klaus Wagenbach, *Franz Kafka: Eine Biographie seiner Jugend, 1883–1912*, p. 149.
10. D-I 44, Feb. 19, 1911.
11. LF 84, Dec. 3, 1912.
12. J 174.
13. D-II 198, Oct. 25, 1921.
14. D-I 268–69, Aug. 16, 1912.
15. LF 35, Nov. 11, 1912.
16. LF 270, June 16, 1913.
17. LF 275, June 21, 1913.
18. LF 295, Aug. 3, 1913.
19. LF 296, Aug. 4, 1913.
20. Br 139, July 1916.
21. LF 417, May 25, 1914.
22. Being a Jewess, Grete Bloch fled to Italy after Hitler had come to power. From Florence she wrote in 1940 to a friend, who later showed Brod the letter, that Kafka, without ever knowing it, had been the father of her son, deceased in 1921, not quite seven years old. It is highly unlikely that the two had met as lovers. During her stay in Florence, Grete Bloch was emotionally disturbed, and in that state might easily have confused the actual father with Kafka whose amorous intentions must have flattered or disturbed her sufficiently never to forget them. Also the dates she mentions make her statement questionable. The unfortunate woman was killed by a German soldier, probably during the deportation of Jews from Italy.
23. Briefe an Felice, p. 598, 11.VI.1914; LF 423, June 11, 1914.
24. D-I 305, Oct. 22, 1913.
25. Klaus Wagenbach, *Franz Kafka in Selbstzeugnissen . . .*, p. 101.
26. LF 508, Sept. 25, 1916.
27. D-II 184–85, Sept. 21, 1917.
28. Br 491.

Chapter Three

1. Br 18, Sept. 6, 1903.
2. Br 21, Nov. 9, 1903.
3. Br 20, Nov. 9, 1903.
4. Br 28, Jan. 27, 1904.
5. All quotations from this little grotesque are taken from Br 14–16, Dec. 20, 1902.
6. Br 29, Aug. 28, 1904.
7. B 58.

8. All quotations from this conversation are taken from B 43–44.

9. LF 31, July 11, 1912.

10. CS 382.

11. Rainer Maria Rilke, *The Notebooks of Malte Laurids Brigge,* p. 15.

12. Rilke says so in a letter to Kurt Wolff of February 17, 1922 (Wolff, *Briefwechsel,* p. 152). It is very likely that Kafka met Rilke in Munich when he gave a public reading of *In the Penal Colony.* He reports to Felice: "Incidentally, back in Prague I remembered Rilke's words. After some extremely kind remarks about *The Stoker,* he went on to say that neither *Metamorphosis* nor *In the Penal Colony* had achieved the same effect. This observation may not be easy to understand, but it is discerning" (LF 536, Dec. 7, 1916).

13. Br 85, Dec. 15, 1910.

14. D-I 133, Nov. 5, 1911.

15. The published version of "Grosser Lärm," omitted in the *Complete Stories,* exists only in German: Franz Kafka, *Die Erzählungen,* p. 253.

16. DF 195.

17. LF 36, Nov. 11, 1912.

Chapter Four

1. D-I 275–76, Sept. 23, 1912.

2. E. T. Beck discusses Kafka's dramatic style in *Kafka and the Yiddish Theater,* pp. 3–11.

3. This stylistic device makes it possible for the author to render a character's thoughts and feelings not as statements of the narrator but from the perspective of that character, thus giving them dramatic effectiveness.

4. CS 77.

5. CS 78.

6. CS 79.

7. CS 81.

8. CS 84.

9. CS 85.

10. CS 86.

11. CS 86.

12. CS 87.

13. CS 87–88.

14. André Gide, *The Counterfeiters,* p. 410.

15. LF 310, Aug. 24, 1913.

16. LF 133, Dec. 29/30, 1912.

17. Ibid.

18. Br 55, perhaps Jan., 1908.

19. D-I 279, Feb. 11, 1913.

20. LF 86–87, Dec. 4/5, 1912.

21. Br 149, Aug. 19, 1916.

22. LF 267, June 10, 1913. What Kafka, not too happily, calls abstractions are the unreal elements of his style, the extended metaphors, blended with the realistic elements. This unusual combination has often been misinterpreted as "a mixture of realism and allegory," as one influential critic, who called the combination "Kafka's peculiar invention," phrased it (Edwin Muir, "Franz Kafka," *Kafka, A Collection of Critical Essays*, ed. Ronald Gray, p. 42).

23. CS 86.

24. D-II 187, Sept. 22, 1917.

25. D-I 278, Sept. 25, 1912.

26. The "early critic" is Kate Flores, author of *The Judgment*. All remaining quotes in this paragraph refer to this work, pp. 14, 23.

27. Wilhelm Emrich, *Franz Kafka*, 1958; Heinz Politzer, *Franz Kafka: Parable and Paradox*, 1962, *Franz Kafka, der Künstler*, 1965; Kurt Weinberg, *Kafkas Dichtungen*, 1963; Walter H. Sokel, *Franz Kafka—Tragik und Ironie*, 1964.

28. Heinz Politzer, *Franz Kafka: Parable and Paradox*, p. 62.

29. Ibid., p. 63.

30. Ibid., p. 61.

31. Ibid., p. 60.

32. CS 87.

33. Heinz Politzer, *Parable and Paradox*, p. 59.

34. LF 115, Dec. 20, 1914.

35. D-II 65, July 23, 1914.

36. Heinz Politzer, *Parable and Paradox*, p. 59.

37. Ibid., p. 60.

38. D-I 279–89, Feb. 12, 1913.

39. Heinz Politzer, *Parable and Paradox*, p. 64.

40. Kurt Weinberg, *Kafkas Dichtungen*, p. 490.

41. Ibid., p. 327.

42. Martin Greenberg, *The Terror of Art—Kafka and Modern Literature*, p. 49.

43. Ibid., p. 54.

44. Ibid., p. 56.

45. Ibid., p. 58.

46. Ibid., p. 57.

47. CS 89.

48. Norman N. Holland, "Realism and Unrealism: Kafka's 'Metamorphosis,' " *Modern Fiction Studies* 4 (Summer, 1958), 145.

49. CS 89.
50. CS 89.
51. LF 414, May 24, 1914.
52. CS 95.
53. D-I 303, Oct. 20, 1913.
54. CS 100–101.
55. CS 91.
56. CS 127. In both translations of *Die Verwandlung*, the German word *Mistkäfer* is incorrectly rendered as "dung beetle." This *Mistkäfer* belongs to the class of characters called: *Mistfink, Miststück, Mistvieh.*
57. CS 129.
58. Johann Wolfgang Goethe, *Italienische Reise*, Vicenza, 19. Sept., 1786. *Werke*, vol. XI, p. 53.
59. Franz Kafka, *Die Erzählungen*, p. 84.
60. CS 130. This is the form in which the sentence is usually quoted.
61. Wilhelm Emrich, *Franz Kafka: A Critical Study of his Writings*, p. 144.
62. Benno von Wiese, *Die Novelle von Goethe bis Kafka*, p. 328.
63. Paul Goodman, *Kafka's Prayer*, p. 95.
64. Stanley Korngold, "Kafka's *Die Verwandlung*: Metamorphosis of the Metaphor." *Mosaic* 3, no. 4 (1970), 104.
65. CS 130–31.
66. CS 136–37.
67. CS 139.
68. Heinz Politzer, *Parable and Paradox*, p. 79.
69. Martin Greenberg, *Terror of Art*, p. 76.
70. "A picture of impudent salacity hangs on his wall . . . a pornographic fetish" (Robert M. Adams, *Strains of Discord. Studies in Literary Openness*, p. 172). "From Kafka's other works it can be inferred that for him fur is almost always the symbol of the female genitals" (Hellmuth Kaiser, "Franz Kafkas Inferno: Eine psychologische Deutung seiner Strafphantasie," *Imago* 20, no. 1 [1931], 59).
71. F. D. Luke, "The Metamorphosis," p. 38.
72. LF 20, Nov. 1, 1912.
73. Ibid., p. 21.
74. Ibid.
75. Friedrich Hölderlin, *Sämtliche Werke*, vol. I, p. 130.
76. CS 383–84.
77. D-II 158, July 6, 1916.
78. A 3.
79. Ibid.

80. Jörg Thalmann, *Wege zu Kafka*, p. 179.
81. A 32.
82. A 54.
83. *Hochzeitsvorbereitungen auf dem Lande*, p. 352.
84. DF 316.
85. A 94–95.
86. A 97.
87. Jörg Thalmann, *Wege zu Kafka*, pp. 156 and 137, also J. Kobs, *Kafka, Untersuchungen zu Bewusstsein und Sprache seiner Gestalten*, p. 42 ff.
88. Mark Spilka, "America: Its Genesis," in *Franz Kafka Today*, p. 112.
89. Ibid., p. 103.
90. A 103.
91. Mark Spilka, "America," p. 113.
92. A 272.
93. A 273.
94. A 280.
95. A 299.
96. Wolfgang Jahn, *Kafkas Roman "Der Verschollene" ("Amerika")*, 1965; Jörg Thalmann, *Wege zu Kafka*, 1966.
97. D-II 132, Sept. 30, 1915.
98. D-II 131, Sept. 29, 1915.
99. LF 138, Jan. 2 to 3, 1913. Two months later he saw this close connection with his inner life only in the first chapter, later published under the title "The Stoker." It had, as he then said, "inner truth," his highest praise for his own productions (LF 218, March 9–10, 1913). Seven years later, he wrote to Milena, the young woman who translated "The Stoker" into Czech, that it was "an abysmally poor story" (LM 24, spring of 1920). In his so-called testament, written January or February, 1922, he exempted "The Stoker" together with his other published stories from the fiery annihilation, decreed for the remaining works. The self-condemnations of this emotional author, particularly in his letters to women, are not lasting judgments.
100. D-II 115, Feb. 9, 1915.
101. Wolfgang Jahn, *Kafkas Roman "Der Verschollene" ("Amerika")*, pp. 145–51.
102. Arthur Holitscher, *Amerika Heute und Morgen*, pp. 100–101.

Chapter Five

1. DF 170.
2. DF 168.

3. D-I 36, Dec. 20, 1910.
4. D-I 129, Nov. 2, 1911.
5. D-II 42, June 6, 1914.
6. D-II 77, July 23, 1914.
7. D-II 77, Aug. 6, 1914.
8. Ibid.
9. D-II 79, Aug. 15, 1914.
10. Br 194–95, Nov. 1917.
11. T 17–18.
12. T 10.
13. Ibid.
14. Ibid.
15. T 17.
16. T 23.
17. BF 56, Nov. 22, 1912.
18. T 297.
19. T 318.
20. Marcel Proust, *Swann's Way*, p. 7.
21. T 319.
22. T 26–27.
23. D-II 114, Feb. 7, 1915.
24. T 57.
25. T 65.
26. T 129.
27. T 135.
28. Walther Rode, *Lesebuch für Angeklagte*, p. 64.
29. T 159.
30. T 158.
31. T 188.
32. D-I 23, July 19, 1910.
33. T 269.
34. Paul Goodman, *Kafka's Prayer*, p. 158.
35. Ibid., p. 160.
36. Ibid., pp. 166–67.
37. Ibid., p. 170.
38. Heinz Politzer, *Parable and Paradox*, p. 177.
39. DF 183.
40. Thomas Mann, *The Magic Mountain*, p. 32.
41. André Gide, *The Counterfeiters*, p. 353.
42. DF 206.
43. T 282–83.

Chapter Six

1. Arthur Schopenhauer, *Parerga und Paralipomena*, vol. II, chap. 12, p. 157.
2. Ben Jonson, *Plays*, p. 445.
3. CS 154.
4. CS 156.
5. Thomas Mann, op. cit., p. 455.
6. CS 167.
7. Thomas Mann, p. 457.
8. Johann Gottfried Herder, *Auch eine Philosophie der Geschichte zur Bildung der Menschheit*, p. 526.
9. Ibid., p. 556.
10. Stefan George, *Der Stern des Bundes*, p. 30.
11. Egon Vietta, "The Fundamental Revolution," in *The Kafka Problem*, p. 340.
12. LF 497, Sept. 10, 1916.
13. Edwin Muir, "Franz Kafka," in *A Franz Kafka Miscellany*, p. 59.
14. J. M. S. Pasley, *Franz Kafka: Der Heizer—In der Strafkolonie—Der Bau*, p. 21. All subsequent quotations about the Old Commandant and the Script are taken from that page.
15. Ronald Gray, *Franz Kafka*, p. 95.
16. Wayne Burns, "In the Penal Colony: Variations on a Theme by Octave Mirbeau," *Accent* 8, no. 1 (1957), 45. Also Hartmut Binder, *Motiv und Gestaltung bei Franz Kafka*, pp. 169–70.
17. Octave Mirbeau, *Le jardin des supplices*, p. 170 (author's translation).
18. D-II 179, Aug. 8, 1917.
19. Jürgen Demmer, *Franz Kafka—der Dichter der Selbstreflexion*, p. 20.
20. Lee Baxandall, "Kafka and Radical Perspective," *Mosaic* 3, no. 4 (1970), 75.
21. Peter D. Webster, "Franz Kafka's 'In the Penal Colony': A Psychoanalytical Interpretation," *American Imago* 13, no. 4 (1956), 399.
22. CS 145.
23. Br 150, Oct. 11, 1916.

Chapter Seven

1. Gustav Janouch, *Conversations with Kafka*, p. 126.
2. CS 415.
3. Robert Kauf, "Verantwortung: The Theme of Kafka's *Landarzt* Cycle," *Modern Language Quarterly* 33, no. 4 (1972), 423.

4. Ibid., p. 425.
5. CS 415.
6. Franz Kafka, *Erzählungen*, p. 154. English translation, CS 401.
7. D-II 187, Sept. 25, 1917.
8. CS 250.
9. Ibid.
10. CS 253.
11. LF 524–25, Oct. 19, 1916. These ideas were very important to him, he copied the letter in his diary, D-II 167, Oct. 18, 1916.
12. CS 258.
13. Franz Kafka, *Erzählungen*, p. 147. English translation, CS 220.
14. D-II 189, Oct. 9, 1917.
15. CS 222.
16. CS 223.
17. CS 222.
18. CS 223.
19. Basil Busacca, "A Country Doctor," in *Franz Kafka Today*, pp. 50–52.
20. CS 224.
21. CS 225.
22. Ibid.
23. Ibid.
24. Ibid.
25. Ibid.
26. Heinz Politzer, *Parable and Paradox*, p. 90.
27. Ibid., p. 89.
28. Walter H. Sokel, *Franz Kafka—Tragik und Ironie*, p. 280.
29. Franz Baumer, *Franz Kafka: Sieben Prosastücke*, p. 112. Also Gert Kleinschmidt, *Ein Landarzt*, p. 119.
30. D-II 182, Sept. 15, 1917.
31. Br 160, Sept. 5, 1917.
32. Hans Egon Holthusen, *Der unbehauste Mensch*.

Chapter Eight

1. LF 546, Sept. 30, 1917.
2. D-I 298, Aug. 21, 1913.
3. D-II 164–65, Aug. 27, 1916.
4. Br 190, Oct./Nov., 1917.
5. Br 235, early March, 1918. What caused this coldness among other things Kafka said in the same letter (p. 236). "I still cannot read the first book of *Either-Or* without aversion." In a previous

letter to Brod he had called this work of Kierkegaard "horrible and disgusting" (Br 224, second half of January, 1918). Two years later he told Janouch: "The *Either-Or* exists only in the head of Sören Kierkegaard. In reality one can achieve an aesthetic enjoyment of life as a result of humble ethical experience" (Gustav Janouch, op. cit., p. 81). Kafka seems to be influenced by Goethe's monistic attitude toward this old problem. In 1828 the old Goethe wrote to Carlyle about the different ethical philosophies, all treating the ethical as incongruous with the aesthetic sphere and concluded: "In the end it seemed most advisable to develop the ethical as well as the aesthetic attitudes from the healthy human nature" (*Goethes Briefe*, Weimar, March 14, 1828, p. 274).

6. Some of the strident self-contradictions in his diaries and letters stem from this dualism, as, for instance, the following: "Coitus as punishment for being together" (D-I 296, Aug. 14, 1913). Nine years later he repeats verbatim Goethe's self-admonition: "Learn, man of forty!" and continues in Goethe's spirit to speak of "the gift of sex" (D-II 203, Jan. 18, 1922). He speaks with puritan, Judaic contempt about the "half naked" Prague women in their summer dresses (Br 405, Aug., 1922), and in the same month he suggests a solution for Brod's marital problems which the young Goethe had chosen as the happy end for the first version of his play *Stella: se mettre en ménage à trois*. Kafka advises his friend to let his wife come to Berlin where the three, the third one being his mistress, should live together "openly—at least among themselves openly" (Br 410, Aug. 16, 1922).

7. Br 315, middle of April, 1921.

8. Søren Kierkegaard, *Fear and Trembling*, p. 49.

9. DF 99–100.

10. Br 252, Feb. 16, 1919.

11. LM 9.

12. Margarete Buber-Neumann, *Kafkas Freundin Milena*, pp. 123–24.

13. František Kautman, "Franz Kafka und die tschechische Literatur," in *Franz Kafka aus Prager Sicht*, p. 74.

14. LM 36.

15. LM 47.

16. LM 223.

17. LM 227.

18. Br 317, middle of April, 1921.

19. B 229–30.

20. Margarete Buber-Neumann, *Milena*, p. 134.

Chapter Nine

1. LM 213.
2. LM 148.
3. CS 449.
4. LM 199.
5. D-II 195, Oct. 19, 1921.
6. The first persecutions of Jews by Christians on a grand scale took place in Spain in the seventh century. The most brutal persecutions began with the first crusade in 1096. With the same poetic freedom which Kafka allowed himself, Heine speaks in one of his poems of having conjured up "the thousand-year-old pain" (Heinrich Heine, *Sämtliche Werke*, vol. I, p. 732).
7. D-II 213–14, Jan. 28, 1922.
8. D-II 214–15, Jan. 29, 1922.
9. DF 37, No. 32. Kafka's aphorisms could not be discussed in this book, dedicated to Kafka the novelist and storyteller.
10. C 12.
11. C 12–13.
12. LM 196.
13. C 13–14.
14. C 17–18.
15. C 21.
16. C 27.
17. C 93–94.
18. C 44.
19. C 51.
20. C 108.
21. C 151.
22. C 437.
23. C 86.
24. C 82.
25. C 96.
26. C 302.
27. C 255–56.
28. C 337.
29. C 67.
30. C 277–78.
31. C 339.
32. C 349–50.
33. In *Amerika*, Karl Rossman had lost his golden opportunity by being too polite to ask his host Pollunder's permission to leave. In

26. Br 487.
27. D-II 31, May 6, 1914.
28. CS 376.

Chapter Eleven

1. The following quotations by Max Brod are contained in the latter's article, "Der Dichter Franz Kafka," *Die Neue Rundschau,* 1921, pp. 1210–16.
2. Albert Soergel, *Dichtung und Dichter der Zeit,* p. 865.
3. Ibid.
4. *Die Literarische Welt,* Dec. 16, 1927.
5. Ibid., Dec. 17, 1926.
6. Max Brod, "Biography of Franz Kafka," excerpted and translated by G. Humphreys-Roberts, *A Franz Kafka Miscellany,* p. 33.
7. Max Brod, *Franz Kafka,* p. 64.
8. *Miscellany,* p. 35.
9. Max Brod, *Franz Kafka,* p. 64.
10. *Miscellany,* p. 35.
11. Ibid.
12. Edwin Berry Burgum, "The Bankruptcy of Faith," in *The Kafka Problem,* p. 305.
13. Ibid., pp. 317–18.
14. D-II 206, Jan. 20, 1922.
15. Paul Reimann, "Kafka und die Gegenwart," in *Franz Kafka aus Prager Sicht,* p. 19. The same misrepresentation of Kafka as a pre-Communist social critic can be found in the only good-sized book about his work which appeared in East Germany. The critic praises the author of *Amerika* for showing "a keenness in his confrontation with various aspects of capitalism, amazing for the time in which the work [*Amerika*] originated" (Helmut Richter, *Franz Kafka: Werk und Entwurf,* p. 188). The work originated when Kafka and other writers of his time were fascinated by the industrial colossus America. Naively, Kafka even wrote his publisher that he had represented "the most modern New York." Although the socialist writer Holitscher was one of his sources, he did not think in terms of proletariat and bourgeoisie but simply in the old terms of poor and rich, the "eternal" contrast in society, as his main inspiration Charles Dickens did. Richter's detailed explanations of Kafka's image of America are dictated by the Communist critic's doctrine, not the novel. He speaks of "the oppressive experiences of unemployed, exploited Karl Rossmann, the servant, tied down like a slave" (Helmut Richter, ibid.). Karl is unemployed only for one night and part of the following

day. During that time he meets two criminal vagabonds, machine fitters, looking for a new employment, but preferring in the end to be kept by Brunelda. They are the source of all of Karl's suffering in the course of the novel. Brutal Delamarche, the proletarian, is the master of the "servant" Karl. Karl's host, kind Pollunder is a capitalist; the unkindness of the bachelors Green and Senator Jacob is the result of their weird characters, not of their class.

16. Richter, Vorwort to *Franz Kafka,* p. 8.

Selected Bibliography

PRIMARY SOURCES

1. German Standard Editions

KAFKA, FRANZ. *Gesammelte Werke.* Edited by Max Brod. New York: Schocken, 1946.
Erzählungen. New York: Schocken, 1946.
Die Erzählungen. Frankfurt a.M.: S. Fischer, 1961.
Hochzeitsvorbereitungen auf dem Lande und andere Prosa aus dem Nachlass. New York: Schocken, 1953.
Beschreibung eines Kampfes. New York: Schocken, 1946.
Amerika. New York: Schocken, 1946.
Der Prozess. New York: Schocken, 1946.
Das Schloss. New York: Schocken, 1946.
Tagebücher 1910–1923. New York: Schocken, 1949.
Briefe an Felice und andere Korrespondenz aus der Verlobungszeit. Edited by Erich Heller and Jürgen Born. Frankfurt a.M.: S. Fischer, 1967.
Briefe an Milena. Edited by Willy Haas. New York: Schocken, 1952.
Briefe 1902–1924. Edited by Max Brod. New York: Schocken, 1958.
Briefe an Ottla und die Familie. Edited by Hartmut Binder und Klaus Wagenbach. Frankfurt a.M.: S. Fischer, 1974.
JANOUCH, GUSTAV. *Gespräche mit Kafka.* Frankfurt a.M.: S. Fischer, 1968.

2. English Standard Editions

The Complete Stories. Edited by Nahum N. Glatzer. New York: Schocken, 1971.
America. Translated by Willa and Edwin Muir. London: Penguin Books, 1949.
The Castle. Translated by Willa and Edwin Muir. Additional material translated by Eithne Wilkins and Ernst Kaiser. London: Penguin Books, 1953.
The Trial. Translated by Willa and Edwin Muir. Additional material translated by Tania and James Stern. London: Penguin Books, 1956.

195

Diaries, 1910–1913. Edited by Max Brod; translated by Joseph Kresh. London: Penguin Books, 1948.

Diaries, 1914–1923. Edited by Max Brod; translated by Martin Greenberg, with the cooperation of Hannah Arendt. London: Penguin Books, 1949.

I am a Memory Come Alive: Autobiographical Writings by Franz Kafka. Edited by Nahum N. Glatzer. New York: Schocken, 1974.

Letters to Felice. Edited by Erich Heller and Jürgen Born; translated by James Stern and Elisabeth Duckworth. New York: Schocken, 1974.

Letters to Milena. Edited by Willy Haas; translated by Tania and James Stern. London: Secker and Warburg, 1953.

Dearest Father: Stories and other Writings. Translated by Ernst Kaiser and Eithne Wilkins. New York: Schocken, 1954.

JANOUCH, GUSTAV. *Conversations with Kafka.* Translated by Goronwy Rees. New York: New Directions, 1971.

SECONDARY SOURCES

Frequent reference is made to the following collections of criticism:

FLORES, ANGEL, ed. *The Kafka Problem.* New York: New Directions, 1963.

————, and SWANDER, HOMER, eds. *Franz Kafka Today.* Madison: University of Wisconsin Press, 1964.

SLOCHOWER, HARRY, ed. *A Franz Kafka Miscellany.* New York: Twice a Year Press, 1946.

ADAMS, ROBERT M. *Strains of Discord: Studies in Literary Openness.* Ithaca: Cornell University Press, 1958.

AUGUSTINUS, AURELIUS. "The Confessions," in *Basic Writings of Saint Augustinus.* Edited by Whitney J. Oates, vol. I. New York: Random House, 1948.

BAUMER, FRANZ. *Franz Kafka: Sieben Prosastücke.* Munich: Kösel, 1965.

BAXANDALL, LEE. "Kafka and the Radical Perspective." *Mosaic* 3, no. 4 (1970), 75.

BECK, EVELYN TORTON. *Kafka and the Yiddish Theater.* Madison: University of Wisconsin Press, 1971.

BEISSNER, FRIEDRICH. *Der Erzähler Franz Kafka.* Stuttgart: Kohlhammer, 1952.

BINDER, HARTMUT. *Motiv und Gestaltung bei Franz Kafka.* Bonn: H. Bouvier, 1966.

BORN, JÜRGEN, DIETZ, LUDWIG, PASLEY, MALCOLM, RAABE, PAUL, and WAGENBACH, KLAUS. *Kafka–Symposium*. Berlin: Klaus Wagenbach, 1965.

BROD, MAX. *Franz Kafka: A Biography*. Second, enlarged edition. Translated by Humphrey G. Roberts and Richard Winston. New York: Schocken, 1960.

————. From "Biography of Franz Kafka." Translated by Humphrey G. Roberts. *A Franz Kafka Miscellany*, pp. 31–38.

————. *Der Prager Kreis*. Stuttgart: Kohlhammer, 1966.

————. *Streitbares Leben*. Munich: Herbig, 1969.

BUBER-NEUMANN, MARGARETE. *Kafkas Freundin Milena*. Munich: Gotthold Müller, 1963.

BURGUM, EDWIN BERRY. "The Bankruptcy of Faith." In *The Kafka Problem*, pp. 305–24.

BURNS, WAYNE. "In the Penal Colony: Variations on a Theme by Octave Mirbeau." *Accent* 8, no. 1 (1957), 45.

BUSACCA, BASIL. "A Country Doctor." In *Franz Kafka Today*, pp. 45–60.

CORNGOLD, STANLEY. "Kafka's 'Die Verwandlung': Metamorphosis of the Metaphor." *Mosaic* 3, no. 4 (Summer 1970), 91–106.

DEMMER, JÜRGEN. *Franz Kafka der Dichter der Selbestreflexion*. Munich: Fink, 1973.

EMRICH, WILHELM. *Franz Kafka: A Critical Study of his Writings*. Translated by S. Z. Buehne. New York: Ungar, 1968.

FLORES, KATE. "The Judgment." In *Franz Kafka Today*, pp. 5–24.

FREY, EBERHARD. *Franz Kafkas Erzählstil*. Bern: Lang, 1970.

GIDE, ANDRÉ. *The Counterfeiters*. New York: The Modern Library, 1955.

GOETHE, JOHANN WOLFGANG VON. *Werke*, vol. XI. Edited by E. Trunz. Hamburg: Wegner, 1964.

————. *Goethes Briefe*. Edited by Karl Robert Mandelkow. Hamburg: Wegner, 1967.

GOODMAN, PAUL. *Kafka's Prayer*. New York: Vanguard Press, 1947.

GRAY, RONALD. *Kafka's Castle*. Cambridge: University Press, 1956.

————. *Franz Kafka*. Cambridge: University Press, 1973.

————, ed. *Kafka. A Collection of Critical Essays*. Englewood Cliffs, N. J.: Prentice-Hall, 1962.

GREENBERG, MARTIN. *The Terror of Art: Kafka and Modern Literature*. New York: Basic Books, 1968.

HAECKEL, ERNST. *Die Welträtsel*. Bonn: Strauss, 1902.

HEINE, HEINRICH. *Sämtliche Werke*, vol. I. Edited by Jost Perfahl. Munich: Winkler, 1969.

HELLER, ERICH, and BEUG, JOACHIM, eds. *Dichter über ihre Dichtungen; Franz Kafka.* Munich: Heimeran, 1969.
HELLER, ERICH. *Kafka.* London: Collins, 1974.
HERDER, JOHANN GOTTFRIED. "Auch eine Philosophie der Geschichte zur Bildung der Menschheit." In *Sämtliche Werke,* vol. V. Edited by Bernhard Suphahn. Berlin: Weidmannsche Buchhandlung, 1892.
HILLMAN, HEINZ. *Franz Kafka: Dichtungstheorie und Dichtungsgestalt.* Bonn: H. Bouvier, 1964.
HÖLDERLIN, FRIEDRICH. *Sämtliche Werke,* vol. I. Edited by Friedrich Beissner and Jochen Schmidt. Frankfurt a.M.: Insel, 1969.
HOLITSCHER, ARTHUR. *Amerika Heute und Morgen.* Berlin: Fischer, 1919.
HOLLAND, NORMAN N. "Realism and Unrealism: Kafka's '*Metamorphosis.*'" *Modern Fiction Studies* 4 (Summer 1958), 143–50.
HOLTHUSEN, HANS EGON. *Der unbehauste Mensch.* Munich: Piper, 1951.
JÄRV, HARRY. *Die Kafka-Literatur. Eine Bibliographie.* Malmö Bolavefors, 1961.
JAHN, WOLFGANG. *Kafkas Roman "Der Verschollene."* Stuttgart: Metzler, 1965.
JENS, WALTER. "Ein Jude namens Kafka." In *Portraits zur deutschjüdischen Geistesgeschichte,* pp. 179–203. Edited by Thilo Koch. Cologne: Du Mont Schauberg, 1961.
KAUF, ROBERT. "*Verantwortung.* The Theme of Kafka's *Landarzt* cycle." *Modern Language Quarterly* 33, no. 4 (1972), 420–32.
KAUTMAN, FRANTIŠEK. "Franz Kafka und die tschechische Literatur." In *Franz Kafka aus Prager Sicht.* Berlin: Voltaire, 1966.
KIERKEGAARD, SØREN. *Fear and Trembling.* Oxford: University Press, 1939.
KLEINSCHMIDT, GERT. "Ein Landarzt." In *Interpretationen zum Deutschunterricht.* Edited by Rupert Hirschenauer and Albrecht Weber. Munich: R. Oldenburg, 1970.
KOBS, JÜRGEN. *Kafka: Untersuchungen zu Bewusstsein und Sprache seiner Gestalten.* Bad Homburg v.d.H.: Athenäum, 1970.
KRUSCHE, DIETRICH. *Kafka und Kafka-Deutung: Die problematisierte Interaktion.* Frankfurt a.M.: S. Fischer, 1974.
LUKE, F. D. "The Metamorphosis." In *Franz Kafka Today,* pp. 25–44.
MANN, THOMAS. *The Magic Mountain.* New York: Vintage, 1969.
MARTINI, FRITZ. "Franz Kafka: Das Schloss." In *Das Wagnis der Sprache.* Stuttgart: Klett, 1954, pp. 287–335.
MIRBEAU, OCTAVE. "Le jardin des supplices." In *Oeuvres illustrée,* vol. III. Paris: Editions Nationales, 1934.

MUIR, EDWIN. "Franz Kafka." In *A Franz Kafka Miscellany*, pp. 55–66.
PASLEY, J. M. S. *Franz Kafka: Der Heizer—In der Strafkolonie—Der Bau.* Cambridge: University Press, 1966.
POLITZER, HEINZ. *Franz Kafka: Parable and Paradox.* Ithaca: Cornell University Press, 1962.
————. *Franz Kafka, der Künstler.* Frankfurt a.M.: S. Fischer, 1965.
PROUST, MARCEL. *Swann's Way.* New York: Vintage, 1970.
REIMANN, PAUL. "Franz Kafka und die Gegenwart." In *Franz Kafka aus Prager Sicht*, pp. 13–44. Berlin: Voltaire, 1966.
RICHTER, HELMUT. *Franz Kafka: Werk und Entwurf.* Berlin: Rütten und Loening, 1962.
RILKE, RAINER MARIA. *The Notebooks of Malte Laurids Brigge.* New York: Capricorn, 1958.
RODE, WALTHER. *Lesebuch für Angeklagte.* Berlin: Transmare, 1931.
SCHOPENHAUER, ARTHUR. "Parerga und Paralipomena." In *Sämtliche Werke*, vol. VI. Edited by Julius Frauenstädt. Leipzig: Brockhaus, 1888.
SOERGEL, ALBERT. *Dichtung und Dichter der Zeit.* Neue Folge: *Im Banne des Expressionismus.* Leipzig: Voigtländer, 1926.
SLOCHOWER, HARRY. "Franz Kafka—Prefascist Exile." In *A Franz Kafka Miscellany*, pp. 7–30.
SOKEL, WALTER H. *Franz Kafka—Tragik und Ironie.* Munich: Langen, Müller, 1964.
SPILKA, MARK. "America: Its Genesis." In *Franz Kafka Today*, pp. 95–116.
STEINHAUER, H. *Die deutsche Novelle 1880–1933.* New York: Norton, 1936.
SWANDER, HOMER. "The Castle, K.'s Village." In *Franz Kafka Today*, pp. 173–92.
TARVER, JOHN CHARLES. *Gustave Flaubert as Seen in his Works and Correspondence.* Westminster: Constable, 1895.
THALMANN, JÖRG. *Wege zu Kafka. Eine Interpretation des Amerika-Romans.* Frauenfeld und Stuttgart: Huber, 1966.
VIETTA, EGON. "The Fundamental Revolution." In *The Kafka Problem*, pp. 340–51.
WAGENBACH, KLAUS. *Franz Kafka. Eine Biographie seiner Jugend.* Bern: Francke, 1958.
————. *Franz Kafka in Selbstzeugnissen und Bilddokumenten.* Hamburg: Rowohlt, 1964.
WEBER, ALBRECHT, SCHLINGMANN, CARSTEN, and KLEINSCHMIDT, GERT. *Interpretationen zu Franz Kafka: "Das Urteil," "Die Verwandlung," "Ein Landarzt," "Kleine Prosastücke."* Munich: Oldenbourg, 1970.

WEBSTER, PETER D. "Franz Kafka's 'In the Penal Colony': A Psycho-
    analytical Interpretation." *American Imago* 13, no. 4 (1956),
    399–407.
WEINBERG, KURT. *Kafkas Dichtungen.* Bern: Francke, 1963.
WELTSCH, FELIX. *Religion und Humor im Leben Franz Kafkas*
    Berlin: Herbig, 1957.
WIESE, BENNO VON. *Die deutsche Novelle von Goethe bis Kafka.*
    Düsseldorf: Bagel, 1956.
WOLFF, KURT. *Briefwechsel eines Verlegers.* Frankfurt a.M.: Scheff-
    ler, 1966.

Index

(The works of Kafka are listed under his name.)

Index